MU...
AND THE
CASTLES OF BAVARIA
in your pocket

Travel Publications

MAIN CONTRIBUTOR: MARTON RADKAI

PHOTOGRAPH CREDITS
Photos supplied by The Travel Library:
15; Andrew Cowin front cover, 5, 6, 12, 17, 23, 24, 26, 27, 28, 29, 31, 32, 33, 34, 37, 38, 40, 42, 44, 45, 47, 51, 53, 54, 58, 59, 60, 66, 67, 68, 69, 71, 72, 73, 75, 77, 82, 84, 85, 86, 87, 97, 102, 108; David Crossland 18, 99; Michael Klinec back cover, title page, 30(t), 35, 41, 43, 46, 48, 56, 62, 64, 65, 78, 89, 91, 105, 107, 111, 123, 125; Marton Radkai 30(b), 61, 76, 92, 98, 117, 118; R Richardson 36, 113.
Other Photos:
Mary Evans Picture Library 10, 14, 20, 21.

Front cover: Mariensäule in Marienplatz, with the tower of the Neues Rathaus and twin towers of the Frauenkirche;
back cover: Neuschwanstein Castle;
title page: fountain at Schloss Linderhof.

MANUFACTURE FRANÇAISE DES PNEUMATIQUES MICHELIN
Place des Carmes-Déchaux – 63000 Clermont-Ferrand (France)
© Michelin et Cie. Propriétaires-Éditeurs 2000
Dépôt légal Jan 2000– ISBN 2-06-653201-0 – ISSN 1272-1689
No part of this publication may be reproduced in any form
without the prior permission of the publisher.
Printed in Spain 02-01/2

MICHELIN TRAVEL PUBLICATIONS
Michelin Tyre plc
The Edward Hyde Building
38 Clarendon Road
WATFORD Herts WD1 1SX - UK
☎ (01923) 415000
www.michelin-travel.com

MICHELIN TRAVEL PUBLICATIONS
Michelin North America
One Parkway South
GREENVILLE, SC 29615
☎ 1-800 423-0485
www.michelin-travel.com

CONTENTS

INTRODUCTION

Munich likes to see itself as a 'world city with a heart'. It seems, however, that most of its residents prefer to call it a 'world village'. This is not merely self-deprecating humour but rather a gentle comment on the fact that it has never lost its small-town flair, its medieval preoccupations, its slightly agricultural and provincial character, its holiday look and feel. The pace is leisurely, *gemütlich* as the Germans say. Being impatient or hectic in Munich can cause the locals to slow down to an unbearably unhurried pace and force you to do as the Bavarians do – take it easy.

The city's incomparable charm lies in its sense of intimacy, of closeness, its accessibility and its bourgeois dignity. Munich was built for walking and looking around, for unwinding and being entertained. It is well-designed and impeccably clean, and the surrounding country unique. Climb up the 'Alter Peter' church tower on a clear day, when the blue sky, as featured on the Munich flag, seems enormous, and you will see snow-capped Alps that seem to be close enough to touch.

Visually Munich still maintains human proportions. Of course modern highrise buildings have appeared since the Second World War – the peculiar piston of BMW, the various Siemens structures, the Olympia centre – but they are not part of the skyline. Since the early 1500s Munich's trademark has been the two towers of the Church of Our Lady; the twin onion domes crowning the slender brick spires have an ever so slightly provincial touch.

At the same time Munich seems to want to

Two bronze lions guard the Felderrnhalle, in Odeunsplutz – one is said to be growling at the Residenz, while the one facing the church is silent.

achieve the unabashed and nonchalant style of the genuine metropolis. It abounds in grand museums exhibiting everything from French Impressionists to antique chamber pots. It has several orchestras of world renown, two opera houses, many concert halls large and small, exhibition halls and a great range of architectural delights past and present. Yet it is so small that any resident walking about the town will inevitably meet friends, acquaintances and business partners. No one can get lost in Munich, not really.

GEOGRAPHY

Although Munich is known for its Alpine backdrop, the city actually stands on a sprawling flat gravel plain. A few kilometres to the south moraine hills rise into the Alps, interspersed with deep, crystal-clear lakes created during the Ice Age. To the north the somewhat harsh gravelly ground gives way to a fertile loamy plain dotted with occasional marshland where groundwater appears on the surface. The city is bisected by the River Isar, which rises in Austria and, despite attempts at regulation, still has the feel of a

mountain stream as it flows through Munich.

Upper Bavaria is very picturesque. The rich soil seems permanently covered by a thick green carpet, which disappears in winter under snow, with here and there stands of pine or mixed species. The local lakes – Tegernsee, Chiemsee, Starnberger See and Ammersee – have cool clear water due, in part, to very stringent sewage control.

HISTORY

Munich's Foundation

The name Munich comes from *Munichen*, meaning monk, but the city owes its actual birth to the coarse yet effective business acumen of the Guelph duke **Henry the Lion**. In 1158 he burned down a bridge over the Isar on the 'salt road', which led from Reichenhall and Hallein, near Salzburg, to Augsburg, and built his own bridge (near where the Ludwig Bridge is today). He established a settlement called '*ze de Munichen*' (meaning 'close to the monks') because it was near a monastery. The Bishop of Freising, who earned good tolls from the first bridge, raised the issue before the Imperial Diet, convened in Augsburg. Emperor Frederick Barbarossa arbitrated wisely: one third of the bridge tolls were to go to Freising, but the town of Munich was given official recognition, with all civic privileges, later even having the right to mint coins.

Rise of the Wittelsbachs

During the Middle Ages Munich – ruled since 1180 by the **Wittelsbach dynasty** – grew

Marienplatz, the heart of Munich, with the Neues Rathaus (right) and Frauenkirche (left). The city stretches away on the flat plain beyond.

7

into a stable little centre of trade. In 1255 Duke **Ludwig II the Stern** (1253-1294) had his residence, the Alter Hof, built in the city. Some 25 years later, Holy Roman Emperor Rudolf gave the people of Munich equal trading rights throughout the Holy Roman Empire. Various religious orders settled in town, notably the Franciscans and the Augustines. In 1306 the Franciscans were granted the right to brew beer and 1328 marks the year the Augustine Brewery (Augustiner-Bräu) was founded. In 1304 the third city seal was designed, with a little monk on it!

The **Golden Age** was introduced by the liberal-minded **Ludwig IV the Bavarian** (1302-1347), who became Holy Roman Emperor in 1328, but the Golden Age came to an abrupt end after his death. A major plague epidemic was followed by a massacre of the Jewish residents. Meanwhile, economic growth – notably the founding of several breweries – had created a strong class of burghers without representation. In 1397 rebellion broke out, and lasted six years before a compromise could be reached.

A certain degree of stability was achieved by **Albrecht IV** (1465-1508), appropriately known as 'the Wise'. In 1506 he introduced primogeniture, which ended the constant partitions and internecine squabbles which usually followed the death of the Duke of Bavaria. Albrecht IV also had the Frauenkirche built by Jörg von Ganghofer, and enacted the Purity Law for beer.

Firm rulers, solid Catholicism, relative wealth and, after 1534, the presence of the Jesuits all contributed to keeping the Reformation out of Bavaria and avoiding the collateral peasant uprisings. Munich began to attract artistic personalities such as Ludwig Senfl, who founded the court orchestra, the sculptor Erasmus Grasser, and later even Orlando di Lasso. The Renaissance, with its secular pleasures, found fertile grounds in the Bavarian capital. A library was established and **Albrecht V** (1550-1579) commissioned the Kunstkammer (Art Chamber), one of the first museums north of the Alps.

Duke Maximilian I, who became Elector in 1623, achieved international recognition by founding the Catholic League in 1609 and by joining the Habsburg side in the Thirty Years War against the Protestants who were led by the Swedish king Gustav Adolph. He also started work on the Residenz, the Hofgarten and other projects, including new defences. On arriving at the gates of the city in May 1632, Gustav Adolph is reported to have described it as a 'golden saddle astride a scrawny nag', a reference to the featureless landscape around Munich. The Swedes burned down a few houses, departing with 42 hostages (who returned soon after). Shortly after the Swedes, Munich was invaded again – this time by the plague, which reduced the city's population by a third, to around 9 000.

Maximilian I's successor, **Ferdinand Maria** (his second name is evidence of the strong Marian cult in Bavaria), married an Italian, Henriette Adelaide of Savoy. She introduced the friendly colours and shapes of the Baroque Age to Munich. The warm yellow Theatinerkirche, one of the gems of Munich, is a product of this glorious epoch.

Unfortunately, the tenure of Duke and Elector **Max Emanuel** was blemished by more war. In 1683 he led his Bavarians

9

against the Turks, who were besieging Vienna, and then pressed on to liberate Belgrade, a difficult, five-year campaign. On the death of his son, Joseph Ferdinand, who was heir to the coveted Spanish throne, a European war broke out pitting Bavaria and France against Austria and England, in which the former were at first victorious. In 1704, however, a Franco-Bavarian army was severely defeated and for the next ten years the Duchy was occupied by the Austrians, while Max Emanuel took refuge in France. Only the peasants in the countryside resisted the occupying Austrian forces; on 25 December 1705, led by a blacksmith from the Upper Bavarian town of Kochel, they marched on Munich, but the good burghers preferred to stay at home while the bedraggled little army was slaughtered near the Sendling Gate.

Karl Albrecht, Duke of Bavaria, was elected Emperor of Germany in 1742 and became known as Charles VII.

The war ended in 1714 with the **Treaty of Rastatt**, and Max Emanuel returned to his city, now poverty-stricken and somewhat run-down. Once again the people were asked to finance a battery of architects, including Cuvilliés, Effner, Gunezrhainer and Fischer, in order to make the city up-to-date, fashionable and beautiful. The Baroque and subsequent Rococo styles were truly Bavarian; something about the odd mixture of humour and earnestness caught the people's fancy. The style was not restricted to the city alone, but reached the deepest recesses of the Bavarian countryside.

Owing to the rise of Prussian power in the north, when Elector **Karl Albrecht**, Duke of Bavaria (1726-1745) became German King and Emperor, Empress Maria Theresa of Austria was not amused; Munich was once again occupied by Austrian troops for a spell.

Enter Napoleon

The Wittelsbach rulers kept a tight hold on their bailiwick during the Enlightenment and Munich attained new artistic heights. **Max Joseph IV**, Duke of Zweibrücken, was in power during the French Revolution. In 1800 French troops occupied the city but six years later, when the Holy Roman Empire officially came to an end, Max Joseph was made King of Bavaria by **Napoleon**, who married his stepson, Eugène de Beauharnais, to August Amalie, Max Joseph's daughter. The deal had been negotiated in part by the wily Count Maximilian von Montgelas, minister of Max Joseph IV. He also switched allegiance after Bavaria lost 30 000 soldiers in the Russian campaign.

With Napoleon came secularisation. Numerous monasteries were put to more social purposes, elementary schools were opened and the state began to institutionalise help for the destitute. New urban plans were drawn up by Karl von Fischer and Friedrich von Sckell to revamp the city, while Leo von Klenze and Friedrich von Gärtner monopolised the architectural trade for the next 50 years and gave the city its sober, classical appearance. As the capital of a fairly liberal kingdom, Munich began to attract many of Germany's leading lights, besides generating some of its own. In 1807 the Viktualienmarkt was inaugurated and in 1811 the first official Oktoberfest was held (*see* p.99).

To an Industrial Nation

The **Industrial Revolution** changed the social fabric of the city, with the founding of the Maffei locomotive factories, the growth of a railway network, steam ships on Lake Starnberg and so on. In the midst of it all, the little monk, the 'Münchner Kindl', reappeared on the city coat of arms and the Weisswurst was invented. As government grew more liberal, something of a modern state started to evolve. Newspapers, literary circles, museums, the theatre and music constituted a solid intellectual base. The

The equestrian statue of Ludwig I was dedicated to the king by the city of Munich in 1862.

University, which had moved from Landshut in 1826, also contributed to the liveliness of Munich life and to the growth of radical movements.

Under **Ludwig I** (1825-48), Munich blossomed into a flourishing university city and centre of art and learning. Ludwig was responsible for much of the imposing architecture in Munich today; the grandiose Ludwigstrasse and Königsplatz were a demonstration of his kingdom's wealth.

Despite this, in 1848 when much of Europe erupted in a bourgeois revolution, the citizens of Munich forced out Ludwig I for his scandalous affair with Lola Montez, the racy dancer, whose full name, Maria de los Dolores Porris y Montez, belied her Irish birth as Elizabeth Rosanna Gilbert.

His successor, **Maximilian II** (1848-64), tried to stabilise the kingdom, by supporting continued economic development and giving Bavaria's agricultural community greater rights. In 1864 the throne passed to **Ludwig II**, the Mad King, (*see* p.14) and by the time he drowned in mysterious circumstances in Lake Starnberg, Bavaria was once again bankrupt and had been forced into the newly-founded German Empire after the Franco-Prussian War of 1870-71.

Under the rule of kings who no longer exhibited much interest, Munich fostered a less austere environment . The New Town Hall was erected between 1867 and 1908, a typical example of vivacious neo-Gothic that embellished the cityscape. Secessionist architects brought their sensual designs to villas and tenements, giving birth to Jugendstil, a German adaptation of Art Nouveau.

'Der Kini'

Bavaria was ruled by many kings and dukes and electors but there was only one 'Kini', a Bavarian dialect for the word *König* meaning king. His portrait can be found all over the place, printed on shirts, on beer mugs and coffee cups,

on postcards and posters, walking-sticks, medals and brooches. Mad King Ludwig II is usually portrayed in profile, with a solemn expression, a perfectly trimmed beard, a well-shaped sensuous mouth, kept in shape by a set of false teeth, and is often dressed in a brilliant blue jacket (his favourite colour). When some older Bavarians out in the country speak of him, there may also be a tearful glint in their eye. Is it genuine sentimentality?

Ludwig was not nearly as much appreciated in his own day, especially by the heavily taxed people of Munich. In 1864, when he became king, he invited Wagner to Munich and lavished huge sums on him for operas that no one really understood. Before long, the people in the city were calling the composer 'Lolus,' a reference to Ludwig I's very costly lover Lola Montez, and Wagner soon took to the hills.

So too did Ludwig. He took refuge in the south, near Füssen, and started to build a series of fantastic fairytale castles – Neuschwanstein and Linderhof and finally Herrenchiemsee on an island in Chiem Lake. In 1870 politics forced him to send Bavarian divisions to fight against the French in the Franco-Prussian war, an abhorrent task for a man who adored French architecture and culture, disliked war and state duties, and who had other ideas as to how and where to spend his and the state's money.

The more he spent on his castles, the lower he sank in the esteem of the people, especially the citizens of Munich. He had no great liking for them and dreaded every occasion when he was compelled to visit the city. Finally, on 10 June 1886, he was declared unfit to rule and his uncle, Prince Luitpold, took over the regency. On 13 June Ludwig II drowned in mysterious circumstances in Lake Starnberg, together with his neurologist von Gudden.

Whatever his state of mind, Ludwig II was the last king of an independent Bavaria and, according to many fiercely patriotic Bavarians with 20/20 hindsight, if he had had his way, the region would still be an independent country.

Left: Mad King Ludwig II.
Below: The 'fairytale' castle of Neuschwanstein.

BACKGROUND

Into the 20C

By the beginning of the 20C, strikes, unrest
and social dissatisfaction had become fairly
common; these tensions were exacerbated
by the First World War. The last of the
Wittelsbach rulers, **Ludwig III**, fled after a
Soviet-style revolution broke out under the
leadership of Kurt Eisner.

In the 1920s Munich lost its cultural
impetus somewhat; hampered by inflation
and prey to all sorts of radical movements, it
no longer seemed master of its own destiny.
By declaring Munich 'the Capital of the
Movement', Hitler made the city a kind of
world pariah. The Münchner Kindl on the
coat-of-arms was given a swastika and in 1936
swastikas also swamped the Oktoberfest. The
very name Munich became a term of
opprobrium in 1938, after the four Heads of
State – Chamberlain, Daladier, Hitler and
Mussolini – signed the **Munich Agreement**
which abandoned Czechoslovakia to
appease Germany.

In 1943 a group of students, Hans and
Sophie Scholl, Alexander Schmorell,
Christian Probst and their philosophy
teacher, Kurt Huber, started to distribute
anti-Hitler leaflets. Although they were all
caught and executed in Stadlheim, this
brave and desperate gesture did something
to salve the conscience of the city during its
darkest days.

Modern Munich

On looking at Munich today it is hard to
imagine the extent of the physical
destruction (not to speak of the human
losses) wrought in the city during the war.
Within a short while, however, the theatres
were reopened (though the Stock Exchange

came first). In 1946 a new Bavarian constitution was enacted and shortly thereafter the Oktoberfest started up again. In 1949, after some hesitation, Bavaria joined the Federal Republic of Germany but kept a separate status – the Free State – which Bavarians of all political colours respect.

The dukes and kings have been replaced by the Minister Presidents, who are virtually always of the conservative Christian Social Union (CSU), which runs a well-oiled political machine in Bavaria. The most famous of its members was the egregious Franz Josef Strauss, long-time Prime Minister and Federal Defence Minister. Munich itself, however, generally votes Social Democrat. It goes its own way, steering a course between radical and petit bourgeois. It is also a highly modern city, the second largest publishing centre in the world, a focus for the electronic media, a German 'silicon valley' and the home of BMW, Siemens and a few other very large corporations. In 1957 it passed the million mark in terms of population but, because building regulations are strict, Munich never gives the impression of being a big city. Its great natural assets are the Alps, the lakes, and the picture-perfect vistas of Upper Bavaria, which make it the most coveted place to live in Germany – and to visit, of course.

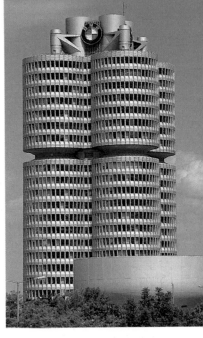

The headquarters of the Bavarian Motor Works (BMW) tower over the bowl-shaped building of the BMW Museum.

PEOPLE AND CULTURE

The '*Ur-Bayer*', the original Bavarian character, is to be found only in the southern reaches of the state, in Upper and to a certain extent in Lower Bavaria. He is notoriously conservative, earthbound, rooted in traditions and rituals that go back centuries. His view of the world – the *Ur-Bayer* is indubitably male – is clear-cut and absolute, and even without an extra beer he will hold forth freely about his neighbours. For example, 56km (35 miles) to the west of Munich live the penny-pinching Swabians. Nürnberg is in Franconia, which begins north of Ingolstadt, and the self-respecting Upper Bavarian will have a few jokes in his snuff pouch about the size of the sausages there. The Franconians around Würzburg, the so-called Booty Bavarians (*Beutebayer*), are named after an obscure historical issue.

Traditional horse-drawn drays deliver special beers to the Oktoberfest.

The rest of Germany is made up of Prussians and beyond them are foreigners, who are of course far more welcome than the Prussians, because the chances of foreigners staying in Bavaria are relatively limited.

People who come to live in Munich or Bavaria are referred to as *Zugeroasten*, which translates best as newcomers. Over the decades, Munich has become a cosmopolitan city but the original Bavarian, with his gravelly dialect, is, of course, still much in evidence. While the natives grumble about the 'Prussians', the latter might remark that without their input, the population of Munich would be less prosperous and influential. They point out that most of the great figures of Munich, from Orlando di Lasso to the chemist Justus von Liebig were, in fact, *Zugeroasten*.

Back to the Future

Whenever Bavarian politicians utter the buzzword innovation, mention of tradition is never far away. The Christian Social Union (CSU), which runs Bavaria, embodies this fascinating mixture of modern capitalism and medieval clericalism, of rude rural cunning and Machiavellian subtlety. The image of the much-feared *Bajuwaren*, wild folk quick to apply the fist when reason no longer prevails, is both denied and cultivated by the Bavarians themselves. But behind the cute *Dirndls* and *Lederhosen*, lies the sharply calculating mind of the *Schlaubayer*, an untranslatable pun referring to peasant cunning. In Munich, the original Bavarians and natives of Munich can be found in the backwaters of Neuhausen, the Westend or in the Au, in the more recondite beer gardens; they may be driving taxis or

19

working behind the counter of the local butcher, baker or grocery store. Though a little hesitant at first, the *Münchner* will be ready to exchange a few words about weather, the Pope, the Stock Exchange, because he or she will always have an opinion, usually a controversial one, for the people like to grumble (*kranteln*)

The Ways and Means of Munich

In order to conceal its provincial aspects, Munich displays an almost exaggerated style in dress, in cars, in architecture. Expensive cars, chic clothing, the right haircut, knowing the right places, are all part of the scene. At many discos, bouncers at the doors keep out undesirables, so that the right crowd can bathe in its own limelight, however dim. This partially explains the Munichers' sometimes unbelievable rudeness, their lack of humour, their reluctance to smile. Indeed, trying to project an image is a strenuous and expensive business. A far greater crime than arriving late for an appointment, by the way, is wearing socks that don't match the rest of your garb.

Culture as a Commodity

At heart, Munich still remains a city of former craftsmen and peasants, who have become solid bourgeois. In terms of the city's past cultural life, we must return to the image of the Bavarian clock. For example, as a composer, Richard Strauss –

Richard Strauss (1864-1949), Munich's greatest composer, eventually became musical director of the city.

perhaps Munich's most famous musical son
– began in a late-Romantic style but, by the
time of his death in 1949, he had turned his
artistic clock back to a form of classicism.
His colleagues – Hans Pfitzner, Werner Egk
and Carl Orff – reveal a similar tendency;
none strayed too far from the straight and
narrow in his compositions, even though
they were unmistakably modern.

By the same token, obtaining good value
for money is what counts, and people do not
scrimp when it is a question of quality. (For
example, Richard Wagner felt the pressure
to leave town in 1865 when, in the opinion
of the people, his output failed to match the
size of his honoraria.) In 1523 Wilhelm IV
invited the then famous composer Ludwig
Senfl to direct the Court's musical life. In

*Richard Wagner was
to revolutionise
German opera by
making the music
secondary to the
dramatic action.*

1556, Duke Albrecht V appointed Orlando di Lasso – probably the greatest composer of the 16C – to the court chapel. As the Baroque age took hold and evolved, Munich's rulers lavished huge sums on architects, painters and stucco artists, who created the beautiful city we see today: from the French-trained Cuvilliés and the local Asam brothers to the incredibly prolific Leo von Klenze. We need not look into the distant past for examples: even in this age of tight budgets, Munich has come up with DM 200 million for its new museum of modern art, the Pinakothek der Moderne, of which 10 per cent was collected in record time from private donations.

Relaxing in front of the Monopteros in the Englischer Garten, the city's playground.

For a while Munich had a true Bohemian district in Schwabing, next to the University. Around the turn of the 20C a host of artists and other creative people, real and bogus, frequented its cafés and salons. Among the most famous were the painters of the *Blaue Reiter* (Blue Rider) movement – Wassily Kandinsky, Franz Marc (known for his horses), August Macke and, for a time, Gabriele Münter and Paul Klee. They were the actual pioneers of abstract painting, but were more or less ignored by Munich society.

As far as literature is concerned, Munich played host to a number of famous people, including Goethe, Rilke, Thomas Mann and Ludwig Thoma, whose criticism of the rulers of Bavaria even earned him a brief spell in prison. He, and others, worked on the satirical magazine *Simplicissimus*, which was read throughout Germany until it closed down voluntarily for patriotic reasons at the outbreak of the First World War. Mention must also be made of the cabaret artists,

from Karl Valentin to contemporary
Gerhard Polt. Unfortunately, they reflect the
fears, obsessions and peculiarities of their
fellow Bavarians so well that they can hardly
be understood beyond the Ingolstadt-
Augsburg line, that is, by Booty Bavarians,
Prussians and other outlanders.

EXPLORING MUNICH

MUST SEE

Alte Pinakothek★★★
Be it as you gaze at a work by
Bosch or Rubens, by Tintoretto
or Altdorfer, at some point as
you wander through the
galleries of masterpieces, the
world outside ceases to exist.

Deutsches Museum★★★
(German Museum)
Science, as it is presented here,
in one of the world's largest
museums, is an exciting and
mysterious journey as you
explore the 17 000 exhibits.

Nymphenburg★★
Home of the rulers of Bavaria:
an elegant **Palace★** and a vast
park★ with swans, ducks, shady
pathways and pavilions that
appear into view as if by magic.
Its **Botanical Gardens★★** are
said to be some of the finest in
the world.

Marienplatz★
This vast square with its

Mariensäule (Marian Statue), the old and new city halls, and shops ranging from traditional Ludwig Beck's to Hugendubel's famous book store is, as ever, the great popular hub of Munich life.

Englischer Garten★
(English Garden)
A 'people's park' designed over 200 years ago, with beer gardens, extensive lawns, a Chinese tower and a neo-Greek temple, and refreshing streams.

Frauenkirche★
(Church of our Lady)
Munich's hallmark church has quietly stood watch over the city since the late 15C.

Glyptothek★
After being greeted by a sensuous Faun, you seem to be walking along the streets of ancient Greece and Rome.

Stadtmuseum★ (City Museum)
Learn about the history of the city, from the brewing of beer to the works of Erasmus Grasser, in these historic surroundings.

Residenz★★ (Palace)
The residence of the Wittelsbachs, first Dukes and later Kings of Bavaria, was begun in 1385 and has evolved over the centuries from a fortified castle to the present splendid palace.

Asamkirche★ (Asam Church)
In this church that they built for themselves, the Asam brothers created a masterpiece of Bavarian Rococo.

Schloss Neuschwanstein★★★
For obvious reasons, Ludwig II's fantasy creation in dazzling white stone is known as 'the fairytale castle'.

Nymphenburg Palace.

ALTSTADT** (OLD TOWN)

It is virtually impossible to capture the character of Munich's Old Town, the area of the city enclosed by the 'Altstadtring' peripheral ring-road, in a single sentence. This part of town bears the traces of every stage of the city's history. It also serves as a repository for contemporary cultural life and consumerism, making it modern, while retaining its old-fashioned and traditional character. Last but by no means least, it bears witness to the undaunted resilience and strength of the city's inhabitants, who managed within only a few decades to restore the ruins caused by extensive bomb damage in the Second World War.

Isartor

The **Isartor** (Isar Gate), featuring a 19C frieze depicting the 1322 Battle of Ampfing, still marks the entrance to Munich as it did in 1337. The gate now houses the

The Isartor was part of the 14C city fortifications built by Ludwig the Bavarian.

Valentin-Musäum (Valentin Museum), which commemorates Karl Valentin, a hilarious and eccentric cabaret artist, who worked in Munich during the first half of the 20C. The museum has adopted the eccentricity of its subject: entrance costs DM 2,99 (99-year-olds with their parents get in free), the museum opens at 10.01am or 11.01 am and closes at 5.29pm, etc.

Munich's other eccentric museum is a few steps from the Musäum, in the narrow side street that leads off to the left from im Tal as you head into town, at no 41 Westenrieder-strasse. The ZAM, **Zentrum für Ausser-gewöhnliche Museen** (Centre for Unusual Museums), was founded by Manfred Klauda, a lawyer with unusual tastes. Perhaps the strangest collections of all are the **Chamber Pot Museum** and the **Bourdalou Museum**, the latter exhibiting examples of a kind of chamber pot used by women in the days of many petticoats and voluminous dresses – and long hours spent at court.

Exhibits at the Chamber Pot Museum.

Medieval Munich

The last vestiges of medieval Munich can be found in this eastern section of the Old Town. In the warren of little streets to the north you'll find the 500-year-old **Dürnbräu** in a house that survived the war, as well as old shops, new restaurants and quite a few sights such as the **Alter Hof** (Old Castle), the first Munich residence of the Wittelbachs, now in the hands of the *Finanzamt* (tax office). The earliest block dates from 1253. Opposite the Hofgraben is the Renaissance **Alte Münze** (City Mint). Another social whirl is the **Platzl**, 'little square', which boasts a Planet Hollywood, an excellent traditional hotel and the world-famous **Hofbräuhaus**. The business has been located here since 1589, but the brewing facilities were moved to bigger premises in the late 19C and the current building extended and rebuilt in 1897.

One of the oldest churches in Munich, Heiliggeistkirche has a lovely Baroque interior by the Asam brothers.

The three-storeyed arcaded inner courtyard of the Alte Münze is a fine example of Bavarian Renaissance.

Im Tal ends at the unpretentious **Heiliggeistkirche** (Church of the Holy Ghost). Originally, the church was part of the city hospital, which is thought to have been founded in 1208. But fire and changing fashions turned it into a Baroque masterpiece (mid-18C) consisting of a single long nave with frescoes and gentle, white stucco work on a pink background by the Asam brothers, Cosmas Damian and Egid Quirin.

Altes Rathaus

The **Altes Rathaus** (Old City Hall), a rather playful construction built in the 1470s by Jörg von Halspach, and which serves as the entrance to

Taking refreshments in the lively and colourful open-air Viktualienmarkt.

Marienplatz, now houses a very well-stocked **toy museum** run by a private individual. It is hard to imagine that it was almost totally destroyed during the war (as was the Heiliggeistkirche), especially when visiting the Council Hall over the archway. The famous morris dancer figures here are copies of the originals by Erasmus Grasser, which can be seen in the City Museum (*see* p.32).

Above left: The famous Hofbräuhaus beer hall in the Platzl.

Left: The Altes Rathaus tower.

Viktualienmarkt (Food Market)

The way to the heart is through the stomach, as the saying goes, so before visiting Marienplatz, by all accounts the heart of the city, time should be set aside for a tour of the **Viktualienmarkt** (literally Victuals Market), Germany's largest regular open-air market.

Anything and everything to do with food can be found here, from tropical fruit, venison, fish and organically-grown foods, to spices, confectionery, bread … the list is endless. The stallholders are generally renowned for their sharp tongues and abrupt manner. The shady Viktualienmarkt, with its little memorial statues to the Eternal Market Woman and the cabaret stars Karl Valentin, Liesl Karlstadt and Weiss Ferdl, is the perfect place for people-watching.

The view from the top of St Peter's church tower can take your breath away.

At the end of Rosental, which runs into Viktualienmarkt, stands the **Stadtmuseum**★ (City Museum). The 'old' section on St Jakobsplatz evolved from an old stable (1410) and the three-story armoury (1493). After the war the museum was rebuilt and partially extended with new buildings. It offers a very broad overview of Munich's history, including works of art, furnishings, documents on traditional folk customs and a number of other subsidiary museums, such as the Puppet Museum and the Museum of Brewing. Do not miss Erasmus Grasser's carved wooden figures, the **Moorish Dancers**★★, on the ground floor.

'Old Peter'

Rindermarkt, the triangular cattle market with a commemorative fountain at its centre, leads past Munich's oldest church, **Peterskirche**, which is known by the locals

simply as 'der alter Peter' (Old Peter). The original late-12C building no longer exists. After heavy bomb damage, Old Peter was rebuilt following plans dating from the mid-17C, with a clover-leaf choir of unplastered bricks. The interior, in the Rococo style, is the work of Ignaz Anton Gunetzrhainer. It has 20 separate side altars, a main altar due in part to the Asam brothers, and a ceiling fresco that is being renovated with the aid of donations. St Peter's most famous feature is its square tower: the platform at the top gives a wonderful **view** of the city, of the goings-on in Marienplatz immediately below, and, if the weather is right, the snow-capped Alps in the background.

The Mariensäule – the point from which all distances in Bavaria are measured.

Marienplatz★ owes its name to the golden **Mariensäule** (Marian Statue), which was erected on the square in 1638, in the midst of the Thirty Years War, to give thanks for delivery from the Protestant Swedes, heresy, hunger and the plague (which had visited the city in 1634). As in the old days, Marienplatz serves as a meeting point for all Munich, and hosts any number of traditional activities such as the Dance of the Schäfflers (coopers), held every seven years since 1683 (its origins are that it allegedly restored people's spirits after a plague). Street musicians and performers also entertain the public, and the playful **Fischbrunnen** (Fish Fountain) in the east corner, which was installed by Konrad Kroll in 1866, is still used to dunk butcher apprentices about to enter professional life. The washing of wallets in the same fountain on Ash Wednesday supposedly ensures wealth. At Advent, the Marienplatz is all aglow with a Christmas market and filled with the tempting smell of hot spiced wine (*Glühwein*) and candied almonds.

Neues Rathaus

A century ago, Marienplatz looked quite different. The Flemish-style neo-Gothic **Neues Rathaus** (New Town Hall) was just

The neo-Gothic Neues Rathaus occupies the entire north side of Marienplatz.

The whole square comes to a halt to hear the 43-bell Glockenspiel.

being constructed and a whole block of houses had to be torn down to make way for the project. Its tall central spire, topped by the **Münchner Kindl** (the little monk), is now an integral part of Munich's skyline. And when its **Glockenspiel** (carillon) rings out across the square (at 11am, noon and 5pm) and the little mechanical figures perform their ritual dance, everyone on the square still stops and looks up. Behind the Neues Rathaus is **Marienhof**, a patch of green where the Jewish ghetto once stood.

Sendlingerstrasse

Sendlingerstrasse, which heads south from Rindermarkt, has a number of interesting shops and the traditional **Hacker** restaurant. In the midst of all this stands the **Asamkirche★**, the private church of the Asam brothers, the famously talented architects, painters and sculptors. Its opulent and expressive frescoes and stucco work seem woven together into a harmonious unit, for the brothers not only drew up the plans but supervised and

35

A magnificent ceiling fresco of the life of St John Nepomuk completes the sumptuous decoration of Asamkirche.

executed the entire building process.

Sendlingerstrasse ends at the old **Sendlinger Tor** (Sendling Gate), which followed the same design as the Isartor until Friedrich von Sckell rebuilt it with a single wide arch.

The streets to the west of Sendlingerstrasse are surprisingly quiet, lined for the most part with simple houses. The **Hundskugel** in Hotterstrasse is the oldest inn in town, dating back to 1440. Allegedly, those condemned to the gallows used to take their last meal here.

Around the Pedestrian Zone

Carved wooden busts of the Apostles, Saints and Prophets, attributed to Grasser, line the choir of Frauenkirche.

Return to Marienplatz and take **Kaufingerstrasse**, Munich's main shopping street, which leads off from Marienplatz and continues as **Neuhauserstrasse**. Between the consumer goods – ranging from clothing, food, souvenirs and towels to hats and sex toys – are some particular treasures. The most immediately noticeable is the **Frauenkirche★** (Church of Our Lady), a tall brick building with two onion-dome towers that was completed at the end of the 15C

and represents the final fling of the Gothic period. It contains fine sculptures from the Grasser workshop. The architect was Jörg von Halspach, also known as Jörg Ganghofer. Legend has it that the devil promised to help Ganghofer if he would build a church without windows. When his work was complete, Ganghofer led the devil to a spot beneath the organ loft from which you could not see any of the windows. The Devil stamped his foot in rage at Ganghofer's guile and left a footprint that all visitors can test for size. From the south tower, a lift takes visitors up to the platform for fine **views**★ of the city.

Bronze sculptures of the Wittelsbachs decorate the façade of Michaelskirche, with St Michael vanquishing Satan between the portals.

Deutsches Jagd- und Fischereimuseum★★
(German Hunting and Fishing Museum)

This spacious museum is located in a building which was originally an Augustine church. It was deconsecrated in the early 19C, served for a while as a customs hall and was then incorporated into the police headquarters. The museum, which includes everything from hunting equipment, paintings of hunting scenes, and the prey stuffed and exhibited, was brought here after reconstruction in the 1960s.

Michaelskirche★

The **Michaelskirche★** (Church of St Michael) is a fine example of Renaissance architecture, clean, sober and symmetrical. From the outside it hardly looks like a church owing, perhaps, to the absence of the tower, which collapsed just before the inauguration of the building in 1590. The project also caused Duke Albrecht to abdicate in the face of bankruptcy. The Jesuits went on to build their college next door. St Michael's is decorated in stucco, though the current work dates from the early 1980s and is somewhat controversial because of some stylistic contradictions apparent only to experts. The **crypt** contains 30 Wittelsbach princes, including Ludwig II.

Almost opposite St Michael's stands the **Augustiner-Bräu**, a traditional Munich beer hall with solid, hospitable tables, food that means business and refreshing beer. The two different façades conceal a single establishment. The arcaded and frescoed inner courtyard is the ideal place to sit in summer, weather permitting. If not, the **Muschelsaal** (Shell Hall) is the last surviving dining room from the days of the regency.

The beer garden in the courtyard of the Augustiner-Bräu, in the centre of town, is one of those hidden surprises that the city reserves for visitors who trouble to seek out its hidden nooks and crannies.

Karlstor

The pedestrian zone ends at **Karlstor** (Karl Gate), which everyone calls the Stachus after the local beer garden 'Stachusgarten', opened by Eustachius Föderl in 1755. This large, semi-circular plaza was reclaimed from a very busy traffic intersection in the 1960s. The large fountain was erected in 1972 and has remained a perennial favourite with dogs, children, teenagers and the inebriated.

To the north of the Stachus are such worthy institutions as the **Palace of Justice**, the **Bavarian Exchange** and the amusing **Künstlerhaus** on Lenbachplatz. The latter was once the club house for the Munich artists' guild. After restoration from its war wounds, it became a restaurant with a small stage and is now run by the international Mövenpick chain. The generous terrace, the ornate interiors, and the coffee and cake certainly make it worth a visit.

Karlsplatz, known as the Stachus, is a popular meeting place. Karlstor can be seen beyond the square.

Around Promenadenplatz

From the Künstlerhaus you can regain the centre of the Old Town by walking down Pacellistrasse, site of the **Dreifaltigkeitskirche** (Church of the Trinity), an unobtrusive monument designed by Giovanni Antonio Viscardi in the early 18C, with frescoes by Cosmas Damian Asam. Being so close to the Residenz, it's no wonder that this entire section of the Old Town is filled with palaces. **Promenadenplatz** is home to, among others, the Dresdener Bank, the HypoVereinsbank and the luxury **Bayerische Hof** hotel which, since 1969, has included the neighbouring **Montgelas Palace**.

Kardinal-Faulhaber-Strasse is somewhat claustrophobic owing to such grand buildings as the **Erzbischöfliches Palais** (Archbishop's Palace) by François Cuvilliés (no 7) and the **Neuhaus-Preysing Palace** in Prannerstrasse. It is quite a relief to reach tiny **Salvatorplatz**, which opens up modestly

Stucco embellishments in the Rococo style feature on the façade of the Neuhaus-Preysing Palace.

onto **Salvator Church**. This began life as a cemetery chapel, and after a long history and near-destruction was given over to Munich's Greek-Orthodox community by Ludwig I in 1829. It is one of the few buildings that only sustained slight damage during the war. Behind it is the **Literaturhaus** (where readings are held) and the **Dukatz** restaurant. Do not be surprised to read such things as 'Mehr Erotik, bitte' (More eroticism, please) at the bottom of your cup. One of the artists at work here was the American Jenny Holzer, whose gimmick is placing double-take statements in double-take locations.

Theatinerkirche★
The massive yellow **Theatinerkirche St Kajetan★** (Theatine Church of St Gaetano), bearing two towers and a cupola, was the fulfilment of a vow by Ferdinand Maria and his wife Henriette Adelaide on the birth of their first son Max Emanuel in 1662. The

The yellow Theatinerkirche is the most prominent building on Odeonsplatz.

The octagonal Brunnenhof (Fountain Court) is dominated by a fountain featuring Duke Otto von Wittelsbach, surrounded by mermen representing Bavarian rivers.

architects were initially Barelli and then Zuccalli. The white stucco decoration on the inside is rich and intricate, but lacks the warmth of the church's fine Baroque exterior. Ludgwigstrasse, which leads off from the sprawling square in front of the Theatinerkirche, is described in the section on Maxvorstadt (*see* p.65).

Residenz★★ (Palace)

If there is any single monument that must be seen in Munich, it is the **Residenz★★** (Palace). Construction of this vast home of the Wittelsbachs began in 1385 under Ludwig V, and evolved into a huge complex of buildings and interior courtyards with private, official, religious and reception rooms documenting architectural and ornamental styles, from the Renaissance to neo-Classicism.

The first museum north of the Alps was founded here when Albrecht V had the **Antiquarium** built, a 69m- (225ft) long barrel-vaulted room that houses antique sculptures. The adjacent **Grottenhof** (Grotto Courtyard) also dates back to the 16C. The next main phase of construction was the **Kaiserhof** (Emperor's Court), which was sponsored by Maximilian I for his own use in the 17C. It included the room now known as the **Steinzimmer** (Stone Room), and the **Vierschimmelsaal** and **Kaisersaal** (Four

Tracing the past in the magnificent Ancestors' Gallery.

Horses Room and Emperor's Room), both of which are used for state receptions. Maximilian commissioned an army of artists to decorate his project with bronzes, tapestries, paintings and frescoes.

The 18C brought one of the finest teams of interior decorators to work their magic on the Residenz: François Cuvilliés the Elder, Johann Dietrich and Johann Baptist Zimmermann, who created, among other things, the **Green Gallery**, the **Ancestors' Gallery** and the **Cuvilliés-Theater★** (or Altes Residenztheater), an intimate little theatre which is still very much in use (*see* p.108). In tribute to Napoleon, who had made him King, Max Joseph commissioned Andreas Gärtner to redesign the **Herkulessaal** (Hercules Hall) and build apartments for his daughter Charlotte, in the Empire style. Finally, Ludwig I invited Leo von Klenze to build the **Königsbau** (Royal Building), which lends Max-Joseph-Platz its sober, classical appearance. Besides its numerous architectural splendours, the building harbours several collections that testify to the combined wealth and taste of the Wittelsbachs, among them the **Schatzkammer★★** (Treasury), which boasts over 1 250 works of art in gold, porcelain and precious stones.

One of the priceless treasures on display in the Residenz's Schatzkammer (Treasury).

Hofgarten
The adjacent **Hofgarten** is almost as old as the Residenz itself. It, too, was destroyed

during the war and rebuilt according to the plans drawn up during the reign of Maximilian I. The French influence is obvious in the geometrical layout. The little temple in the middle is thought to be by Heinrich Schön. In the 1980s, the Bavarian government decided to build itself a new Chancellery using the surviving cupola of the old neo-Renaissance Army Museum. Architect Diethart Siegert essentially added two long wings, not unlike the original, except that they are of glass and steel. This imposing edifice was promptly baptised Palazzo Prozzo (which translates more or less as 'Show-off Palace') by the people of Munich.

Maximilianstrasse

Maximilianstrasse is Munich's most exclusive street, with expensive galleries and shops, the luxury **Vier Jahreszeiten Hotel** (a Kempinski hotel), which has been in business since 1857, and chic Schumann's Bar. Maximilian II had this smart avenue

Maximilian I greets visitors to the Nationaltheater.

The monumental Maximilianeum, seat of the Bavarian Parliament and its Senate.

built as a monument to himself. It begins at Max-Joseph-Platz, where Klenze's hand is still very much in evidence, not only in the Residenz, but also in the **Nationaltheater** (National Theatre). The theatre, designed by Carl von Fischer with an orderly Classical colonnade, replaced the old Franciscan monastery that once stood here. After a fire in 1823, Klenze added the second decorated tympanum, lending the theatre a slightly more playful aspect. It is home to the Bavarian National Opera.

Beyond the Old Town limits, Maximilianstrasse becomes an even more extravagant monument to its builder, King Maximilian II. To the left stretches the neo-Gothic façade of the **Government Building of Upper Bavaria**, built between 1856 and 1864 by Friedrich Bürklein. Opposite is the **State Ethnological Museum** by Eduard Riedel, which documents all world cultures (except European), and almost always hosts a special exhibition. Maximilianstrasse splits to form an island on which a bronze statue of Maximilian II stands, depicting the ruler in all his glory, surrounded by his buildings. In the background, resting comfortably on the elevated right bank of the Isar, is what Maximilian intended to be his great pedagogical masterpiece, the **Maximilianeum**. It became the convention hall for the Bavarian Senate.

ALONG THE ISAR

The River Isar does not cut Munich equally in two. The city seems to have kept most of its important sights jealously on the left bank, where it was born, and they are mostly 'inland'. This was partly for reasons of protection. The Isar can rise to impressive heights, but without any danger to the houses along its banks.

Tierpark Hellabrunn★

When **Tierpark Hellabrunn★** (Hellabrun Zoological Gardens) was opened in 1913 in the south of Munich (6km/4 miles from the centre; U-Bahn Thalkirchen), it was the biggest zoo in the world. Time has downsized it somewhat, but it may well still rank as one of the most beautiful. Great care was invested in the architecture, from the Moorish elephants' house to the 'tent roof' over the aviary and tigers' house, which reveals the Frei Otto touch.

Next to the Zoo is a stretch of the Isar called **Flaucher**, a series of islands and peninsulas formed by the river at the foot of a dam where people flock in their hundreds in the summer to celebrate sun and water.

The Isar still has the feel of a mountain river as it flows through Munich.

The Au

The right bank of the Isar maintains its recreational aspect well into town. By Wittelsbacher Bridge lies the **Schyrenbad**, a pleasant open-air pool with clean lawns and modern facilities. The Au more or less begins here, a district of Munich first documented in 1289 that still reveals its working-class past, with rows of small houses in narrow streets. At the centre is the generously-proportioned **Mariahilfplatz**, with the simple but unequivocally majestic **Mariahilf Church** of plain brick, the work of Joseph D Ohlmüller and Georg F Ziebland. Besides the regular Wednesday farmers' market, Mariahilfplatz hosts three special commercial events (and has done since 1310!): the *Auer Maidult* (Dult is an old word for market) in April, with potters, fast-food stands and some excellent bric-à-brac, and a repeat performance at the end of July (*Jakobidult*) and in October (*Kirchweihdult*).

Thalkirchen and Glockenbach

Thalkirchen could be described as the stomach of Munich. The central wholesale markets and the slaughterhouse are located here, on either side of the **Südbahnhof** (south rail station), which is only used for freight. This guarantees the district a certain raw liveliness.

Heading north towards the centre, you arrive at a far quieter residential area that begins – no irony intended – with the **Alter Südlicher Friedhof** (Old South Cemetery), final resting place of a number of important Munich residents, including the painters Carl Spitzweg and Moritz von Schwind, and some of Munich's most important architects – Gabriel von Seidl, Friedrich von Gärtner and Leo von Klenze.

The **Glockenbach** district, named after the Glocken stream running through it, has become a highly popular residential area in the past decade. The little 'shops next door', which used to cover every household need, have for the most part given way to chic fashion boutiques, cheap interior decoration stores and dozens of shops selling spiritualists' accessories – from eagle feathers to mass-produced native American dream catchers. Klenzestrasse leads straight to a quarter that was built up during the mid-19C and has been named after the **Gärtnerplatz**, a pretty, circular square with a fountain in its middle. The **Gärtnerplatztheater**, which occupies one slice of the pie as it were, was originally opened in 1865 as the **Aktien-Volkstheater** (People's Theatre Corporation). It is now a state-run operation. The Gärtnerplatztheater has never lost sight of its 'popular' mission – prices are affordable and the programme ranges from

Display of locomotives, Deutsches Museum.

such works as Lortzing's *Der Wildschütz* and Mozart's *Gärtnerin aus Liebe*, to Bernstein's *West Side Story*.

Deutsches Museum★★★

The **Deutsches Museum★★★**, on the island in the Isar (Museumsinsel), was the brainchild of the engineer Oskar von Miller, who wished to exhibit the 'masterpieces of natural sciences and technology'. The entire complex was built, extended and rebuilt between 1906 and 1993, and incorporates a library, the planetarium, exhibitions covering aircraft, trains, cars, shipping, mining, physics, space travel, and much more. Of course, many of the exhibits can be 'tried' by the visitors, with plenty of hands-on activities to keep youngsters entertained, and the museum usually has

some special temporary exhibition on offer. A very popular component of the Deutsches Museum experience is the giant **IMAX** projection screen in the Forum der Technik.

The front of the Deutsches Museum is on Ludwig Bridge, which is located approximately where Munich's first bridge was built (*see* p.7). Across the bridge is a small shady square with the **Vater-Rhein-Brunnen** (Father Rhine Fountain). A weir connects Museum Island to the Prater Island, where the Alpine Club's **Alpine Museum** is housed in a neat little 1888 mansion.

Haidhausen

The district of Haidhausen leads off onto the right-bank from the foot of the Ludwig Bridge. It is a lively area, favoured by artists, with ethnic shops, restaurants and cafés, and an atmosphere reminiscent of that once found in Schwabing. Immediately to the left of the Ludwig Bridge is a gift to Munich's people by the civilian engineer Karl Müller, the **Müllersches Volksbad** (Müller's Public Bath), which was built between 1897 and 1901 by Carl Hocheder. Stylistically, the building is a mixture of neo-Baroque, neo-Roman and Jugendstil. The splendid interior was very carefully restored in the early 1990s.

Behind the Baths on a spit of land pointing into the Isar is the old city wellhouse, which was later expanded to house an electrical plant. Since the early 1990s, the **Muffathalle** (Muffat Hall) has served as a cultural centre, with a regular café and a programme of mainly popular musical events. Munich's more classical cultural centre, however, is simply called the **Gasteig**, a huge, looming brick building at the junction of Rosenheimerstrasse and Wienerstrasse.

Müllersches Volksbad, the 'people's baths' (right), are housed in an impressive Jugendstil setting next to the River Isar.

The building's sheer mass is relieved to some extent by the unusual angles and the collection of tall, flamboyant windows facing the river. The Munich Philharmonic has its home here, as do the main public library, the Richard-Strauss Conservatory, the contemporary Black Box stage and a few other institutions. Every now and then, an exhibition is held in the area on the first floor.

On the same street stand the massive offices of the GEMA (the powerful German society of music authors), in front of which is an amusing musical instrument fountain designed by Albert Hien, consisting of a larger-than-life-size trumpet and piano.

The **Hochstrasse**, which surrounds the

Motorama shopping centre (arguably one of the ugliest buildings in the whole of Munich) eventually leads to the **Paulanerkeller**, home to a typical beer garden beneath chestnut trees and birthplace of Salvator, the dark beer brewed during Lent (*see* p.98).

When Haidhausen was recently discovered by the speculators and the smart set, many old Haidhausers felt the neighbourhood lost its essential character. On the other hand, the influx of money, combined with a new awareness of the importance of conserving existing buildings, is having a visibly positive effect on the quarter. It was the city, however, that restored some of the last **Herbergen**, little 'hostels' for the less privileged people that were often paid for by the wealthy and built on plots that had no economic potential, i.e. on slopes or in damp areas. The log cabin (**Kriechbaumhof**) on Preysingstrasse is a replica, the original

The log cabin (Kriechbaumhof) on Preysingstrasse, a reminder of Haidhausen's past.

The cobbled stretch of Preysingstrasse, with its view of the old monastery, has something magical about it.

having burned down, and opposite is the **Übelackerhäuschen**, which is used as a potter's studio. At no 24 Kirchenstrasse is the **Museum of Haidhausen**, with temporary exhibitions relating to the district's history.

To the north of Haidhausen is Johannis-Platz, named after its tall, red-brick church, and next to this is **Wienerplatz**, which has a rather over-slick 'in' café and a far more genuine **Hofbräu** beer-hall-cum-beer-garden. The maypole poking out of the handful of market stalls on the little square gives the place a village-like atmosphere that is drowned out only by the steady traffic heading to and from the city centre on the Innere-Wiener-Strasse.

PRINZREGENTENSTRASSE

Right Bank

In spite of its name, Regent Street, and its lofty status as one of Munich's main avenues, **Prinzregentenstrasse** did not evolve in the same organic fashion as Maximilianstrasse and Ludwigstrasse. Starting on the right bank of the Isar, it seems to have developed in fits and starts before running out of energy somewhat. Much of Bogenhausen, the 'posh' quarter that begins at this point, testifies to this, with opulent villas rubbing shoulders with ordinary family houses.

One initiative intended to fire up the energy of east Munich was the construction of the **Prinzregententheater** by Max Littman, at the beginning of the 20C, a job for a building society of which he was a member. It still puts on a regular programme, but its true heyday was between 1945 and 1963, while the national Operahouse was being restored. (A visit to **Käfer**, a few blocks to the west, is a must: it's the headquarters of Germany's most successful caterer – but is not cheap, however!)

The artist **Franz von Stuck** had an exotic late-19C villa, **Villa Stuck**, built on the avenue. His murals, sculptures and paintings are still in place, including the amusing *Dissonanz* (Dissonance), which features a baby Pan trying to play a pan flute with an adult of the species holding his ears in horror. The Museum Stuck otherwise hosts temporary exhibitions. A major extension project is currently in progress and is scheduled to be completed in 2002.

The spear-throwing bronze Amazon in front of the Villa Stuck was based on a design by Stuck.

In the middle of the avenue is the **Friedensengel** (Angel of Peace), a radiant gilded copy of the Nike of Paionios at the top of a 38m (125ft) column. Few ever bother to look at the base, a hall of fame to the German emperors and the Wittelsbach monarchs, to Bismarck, Moltke, Roon, von der Tann and others who participated in the Franco-Prussian War of 1870-71.

Left Bank

Crossing over the Maximiliansbrücke into the district of **Lehel**, Prinzregentenstrasse is perfectly divided, with government buildings on the left (the south side) and museums on the right. The first building at the corner of Reitmoserstrasse is the former residence of the Prussian ambassador and the **Schackgalerie**★, housing the remarkable art collection that Prussian Count von Schack donated to the city. This includes works by Böcklin, Feuerbach, Moritz von

Schwind and Carl Spitzweg.

A little further along the street stands Gabriel von Seidl's sprawling **Bayerisches Nationalmuseum★★** (Bavarian National Museum), covering a broad spectrum of Bavarian arts and crafts from various periods, wood carvings, pottery, paintings, traditional peasant artefacts and a superb collection of nativity scenes. One section is devoted to 20C applied arts and industrial design. Munich's **Prähistorische Staatssammlung** (Prehistoric Collection), with an exhibition covering the period from the Stone Age to the early Middle Ages, is located in a modern building behind the Bavarian National Museum (entrance on Lerchenfeldstrasse).

The last museum is the **Haus der Kunst**, a typical National Socialist construction (by Paul Troost) with a neo-Classical façade. It has its own exhibition of modern paintings, the **Staatsgalerie Moderner Kunst** (Modern Art Collection), housed in the west wing, but is generally used for temporary exhibitions.

Prinzregentenstrasse disappears into a tunnel, which almost passes under the **Prinz-Carl-Palais**, the official residence of the Bavarian Minister President. It was named after its first inhabitant Prince Carl, the brother of Ludwig I. To the south is **St Anna-Platz**, which has been carefully paved and restored. An Italian delicatessen-cum-café and restaurant, with the un-Italian name of **Gandl**, is a most inviting place for excellent coffee and a bite to eat. The only competition on the little square, in the shadow of St Anna Church, is the Café Wünsche, which offers a long display case of pretty serious cakes and some ornate marzipan *objets d'arts*.

MAXVORSTADT

The great museums, the Ludwig-Maximilian and Technical Universities are located in the district called **Maxvorstadt**, the area more or less between the axes of the rail tracks and Ludwigstrasse, which runs from the **Feldherrnhalle** (Hall of the Generals) as far as the **Siegestor** (Victory Gate). In 1807, Elector Max Joseph IV, who had just become King Maximilian (Max) I, commissioned Friedrich von Sckell and Karl von Fischer to redesign this area of the growing city. Leo von Klenze, undoubtedly Munich's most prolific architect, was put in charge of designing the ensemble around Königsplatz.

A good place to begin is at the **Platz der Opfer des Nationalsozialismus**, where an eternal flame burns in a huge cubical cage as a memorial to the victims of Nazism. To the left is **Maximilianplatz**, which is often mistaken for merely a green strip dividing the Altstadtring (the peripheral ring-road around the Old Town). In fact it is a small

The triumphal Feldherrnhalle serves as a war memorial to those who fell in the Franco-Prussian War of 1870-71.

park with very fine gilded statues of Johann Wolfgang von Goethe, Friedrich Schiller and the two chemists, Justus Liebig and Max von Pettenkofer. At the southern end of the plaza is the grandiose **Wittelsbacher Brunnen** (Wittelsbach Fountain), the work of Adolf von Hildebrand in 1895.

Karolinenplatz

Briennerstrasse leads to Königsplatz, passing through Karolinenplatz, a perfectly circular plaza with a 29m- (95ft) high **Obelisk** at its centre, designed by Leo von Klenze. It was clad with iron plates cast from the Turkish cannon captured at the 1827 naval battle in the Bay of Navarin, during the Greek War of Independence. Immediately to the right, down Arcisstrasse, is the **Hochschule für Musik** (College of Music), a typical example of Nazi architecture. From time to time the students give excellent concerts and recitals, for which there is no admission charge.

An obelisk marks the centre point of the circular Karolinenplatz.

Königsplatz

When the early-morning sun gilds the
Propyläen that closes off Briennerstrasse, it
creates a magical scene. To the right and left
respectively stand the **Glyptothek★**
(Sculpture Gallery) and the **Staatliche
Antikensammlungen★** (State Antiquities
Collection), built by Georg Friedrich
Ziebland, a pupil of von Fischer. The three
buildings reflect the evolution of Greek
architecture, as replicas spanning the Doric,
Ionian and Corinthian styles.

Staatliche Antikensammlungen★

The Antiquities Collections evolved out of
Ludwig I's collection of Attic and Etruscan
art, the Royal Antiquarium and a few private
collections. Over 600 vases and other vessels
are exhibited on the ground floor of the
museum (currently being reorganised). The
lower level of the Antikensammlung
presents a wide variety of objects, from

*Looking across the
Classical
Königsplatz to the
Glyptothek
Museum.*

For a special treat, and one unique to Munich, take a coffee break in the Glyptothek's Sphinx Room, or in the quiet of the courtyard with its greenery and scattered sculptures, on a warm summer's morning.

A thousand years of Greek and Roman sculpture are displayed in the Glyptothek.

glassware to a series of 19C replicas. Amid the collections of helmets, fibulae, Etruscan jewellery, cast bronze figures and diverse fragments, is a small collection of medical instruments that will make you thankful for the advances of modern medicine.

Glyptothek★

Like the Antikensammlungen, the Glyptothek opposite was the brainchild of Ludwig I, who also started the collection of sculptures it houses. It was built from 1816 to 1830 under the direction of Leo von Klenze, and remains to this day one of the most beautiful museums of Antiquities in Germany. It houses Roman and Greek sculptures arranged in spacious halls surrounding an inner courtyard. The gentle, indirect light bathing the works almost makes them come alive, especially the **Barberini Faun**, unabashedly naked and sensuous, who greets the visitor on entering. The

tympanum figures from the **Temple of Aegina** are among the great treasures here. In the **Hall of Roman Portraits**, there is a complete mosaic from a villa, depicting a sun god in a Zodiac wheel and an earth goddess with the four seasons as her children.

Lenbachhaus

The former home and studio of Franz von Lenbach (1836-1904) is located on Luisenstrasse, just a few steps from the Propyläen. It was built between 1887 and 1891 by architect Gabriel von Seidl, but was later extended to accommodate a gallery. You can easily get lost inside the **Städtische Galerie im Lenbachhaus★** (Lenbach Collections), as it is officially called today, which is devoted to 19C Munich painters. Staircases lead to remote corners where modern works and exhibits suddenly and

Take a rest in the shady courtyard of Lenbachhaus after admiring the 19C paintings in its galleries.

incongruously appear. Upstairs are five original rooms, which were renovated in the mid-1990s by the Münchner Werkstätten. And, of course, you will find the largest collection of paintings from the members of the **Blaue Reiter** (Blue Rider) – Wassily Kandinsky, Franz Marc, Gabriele Münter, Alexei von Jawlensky and others.

Also not to be missed at the Lenbachhaus is the 120m (395ft) **Kunstbau** (Art Building), located in a tunnel that was left over when the U-Bahn was built under Königsplatz.

Alte and Neue Pinakothek★★★

These two art galleries are the finest gems in Munich's cultural crown. The **Alte Pinakothek★★★** was built by Klenze just after the Glyptothek, also a commission by Ludwig I. It was heavily damaged during the war and was repaired with great economy, leaving the scars visible to this day. This huge gallery, which is almost 137m (450ft) long, now stands on a pleasant green square that is populated by sun-seekers in summer or by impromptu soccer players. Inside is a vast wealth of nearly 9 000 paintings by European artists ranging from the 15C to the 18C, including such names as Rubens, Bosch, Bruegel (the Elder), Tintoretto, Lucas Cranach and Albrecht Dürer. Among the fine works here is Tintoretto's *Portrait of Emperor Karl V*, Rubens' wonderful *St Christopher* and a self-portrait by Dürer.

Ludwig I's **Neue Pinakothek★★** was so badly damaged in the war that it had to be demolished and replaced with a sandstone post-modernist style building, designed by Alexander von Brancas. The quality of the 19C and early 20C paintings in the spacious

The post-modernist style Neue Pinakothek houses an outstanding art collection.

rooms show that Ludwig I, who started the collection, was a genuine patron of the arts. This museum now includes the French Realists (Millet and Géricault), the 'Deutschrömer,' German artists such as Böcklin and Feuerbach, who made Italy a central element of their work, the Classicists, the Impressionists (Monet, Manet, van der Velde), and finally the Secessionists, Symbolists and post-Impressionists such as Cézanne and Gauguin.

Taking a break on the terrace of the museum's Italian restaurant is one option after a visit. The **Brasserie Tresznjewski**, on the corner of Arcisstrasse and Barerstrasse, is the place to pause and watch a somewhat chic-conservative crowd unwinding.

Opposite the Alte Pinakothek is Munich's pride and joy, the brand new **Pinakothek der Moderne**, which will house the collections from the State Gallery of Modern Art, the New Collection (including industrial graphic design and crafts), the Architectural Museum and the State Graphics Collection. It is scheduled to open in summer 2000.

Ludwigstrasse

The entire 'nucleus' of Maxvorstadt beyond the museums consists of a lively student quarter that is best visited as part of a leisurely stroll. The focal point is Amalienstrasse, Türkenstrasse, Schellingstrasse and Arcisstrasse. The eastern boundary is the magnificent Ludwigstrasse, leading off from the **Feldherrnhalle** (Hall of the Generals; *see* p.58).

Leo von Klenze was put in charge of the first section of the avenue in 1817, but was replaced by Friedrich von Gärtner in 1830, hence the two different styles. For **Odeonsplatz**, at the beginning of the avenue, Klenze borrowed from the Italian Renaissance, building large, symmetrical, sober houses. Along the western edge of the Hofgarten is the one-time **Bazar** building, which houses the traditional **Tambosi** café. On the east side is the impressive **Bavarian State Chancellery**.

Four great masters of learning – Hippocrates, Aristotle, Homer and the Athenian historian Thucydides – outside the Bayerische Staatsbibliothek.

Friedrich von Gärtner's work begins around the **Bayerische Staatsbibliothek** (State Library), known popularly as the 'Stabi'. Four statues outside – of Hippocrates, Aristotle, Homer and the Athenian historian Thucydides – announce it. The Ludwigstrasse might seem monotonous were it not for the **Ludwigskirche** (Ludwig Church), whose two Romanesque spires can be seen beckoning from some distance. In comparison to Bavaria's famous Baroque churches, the Ludwigskirche seems almost Spartan, with its figurative ornamentation. The three

One of Gärtner's fountains, with Ludwigskirche beyond.

frescos are especially impressive. Peter Cornelius' depiction of *Judgement Day* on the cloister wall is the largest, after Michelangelo's work in the Cistine Chapel.

The avenue then opens onto a square graced by two fountains and surrounded by the main buildings of the **Ludwig-Maximilians-Universität**, before ending at a Victory Gate with a quadriga, the freshly restored **Siegestor**. Heavily damaged during the war, the monument was restored by 1958 and now bears the inscription 'Dedicated to victory, destroyed by war, admonishing peace.'

The Siegestor, the triumphal arch erected by Ludwig I.

Olympiapark

Before Franz Josef Strauss and Riem were built, Munich's airport was located at the Oberwiesenfeld, between Schwabing and Neuhausen, a broad meadow once used for races and other entertainment. Small aeroplanes landed here, as did massive Zeppelins. Gustav Otto pioneered flights over the field and the budding BMW company tested its flying machines. The war swept away the Oberwiesenfeld, and within a few years the rubble from the destroyed city was piled up here, next to the ruined buildings of Munich's first airport.

Timofei Prokhorov and his companion Natasha, who had been displaced from Russia by the war, settled here. Timofei was told by the Virgin Mary in a dream to build a church. This he did, using bricks from the destroyed city. For tapestries and fabric furnishings, he and Natasha used the wool from old pullovers.

For the 1972 Olympics, the rubble was properly landscaped. Nestling in these 'hills' today are the lake, with the stadium, **Olympiahalle** (auditorium) and pool all under a single tent-like roof of plexiglass and steel – an incredible futuristic vision by architects Behnisch and Otto, which has lost none of its beauty. A little further off are the cycling stadium and the ice rink. The 290m- (950ft) high **Olympiaturm** (television

Left: The Olympiaturm.
Right: Aerial view of Olympiapark.

tower), which offers a terrific **view★★**, was built in the late 1960s. Just beyond it, the 'four-cylinder' **BMW headquarters** and **museum** was completed in time for the Olympics (*see* p.72).

Timofei and Natasha were almost bulldozed out of existence, but the people of Munich expressed their anger, and the two hermits were allowed to remain.

The Olympiapark is now a bustling place, with joggers, cyclists and walkers, sunbathers and even skiers and people sledging in winter. The old sports halls are used for a variety of events, notably football matches and big pop concerts. The ice rink now includes a roller-blading rink, and the cycling stadium has been turned into Olympic Spirit, the world's first interactive theme park focusing on the Olympic sports.

Timofei still lives here at the age of 105 (in 1999). Natasha died in 1975. People visit the chapel and museum that tells the story of their hermitage and the Oberwiesenfeld.

SCHWABING

Schwabing, the old artists' quarter, begins just north of the Siegestor at the entrance of the **Akademie der Bildenden Künste** (Academy of Fine Arts), a pompous neo-Renaissance construction by Gottfried von Neureuther, which more than reflects its reputation in the 19C as a bastion of conservatism. Visitors to the Academy are greeted by a starkly contrasting oddity in the shape of the enormous *Walking Man* by Jonathan Borofsky, which puts things back into perspective.

No more than a village 150 years ago, Schwabing began attracting artists and all manner of creative people in the second half of the 19C, siphoning energy from the University. As such, it became the driving force behind Munich's cultural life and a symbol for the bohemian, for alternative lifestyles, for unconventionality. Schwabing's old reputation dies hard, but the less charitable might claim nowadays that there is less to Schwabing than meets the eye. Indeed, the **Leopoldstrasse** is something of a catwalk for those who like to be seen. Most cafés, it seems, have been refurbished for the energy-drink crowd with pierced bodies, tattoos and trendy dreadlocks. This is fun to watch for a time, but rapidly becomes monotonous.

Münchner Freiheit, a large square in the district's middle, was named after an anti-Nazi resistance group. Cafés sprawl as far into the square as zoning laws allow, and market stands are beginning to make an appearance. The lively, asymetrically decorated Jugendstil house on the west side of the square was designed by the

A colourful example of Jugendstil architecture on Ainmillerstrasse.

Hungarian architect Ödön Lechner. The narrow streets to the east of Münchner Freiheit are lined with the ubiquitous *Kneipen*, pubs for all tastes, as well as shops and restaurants. **Occamstrasse**, in particular, is renowned as Munich's 'longest bar'.

Among the other interesting squares in Schwabing is **Kurfürstenplatz**, where the **Café Schwabing** attracts a mixed in-crowd of students and professionals. Further south is **Elisabethplatz**, tucked between the **Schauburg Youth Theatre** and the spectacular **Berufschule** (Vocational College), which was completed by Theodor Fischer in 1901. This shady square boasts a friendly market for groceries, meat, cheese, fish, bread, flowers, etc. To the west lies **Hohenzollernplatz**, which has a loudly

gushing fountain in its centre. Around the corner is the **Nordbad** (North Baths) with a swimming pool, a typical National Socialist construction that was restored after the war and entirely revamped and modernised in the early 1990s. **Josephsplatz**, to the south of Hohenzollernplatz, is little more than a playground in the shadow of **St Joseph Parish Church**, a huge yellow building with a very simple, white interior. On warm summer days, people enjoy their lunch breaks in Schwabing's **Alter Nördlicher Friedhof** (Old Northern Cemetery). On tiny Zieblandstrasse is the unique **Gallerie Bìro**, a gallery exhibiting high-quality jewellery made of alternative materials.

Nostalgic exhibits in the BMW Museum, at its headquarters near the Olympiaturm.

ENGLISCHER GARTEN★

Munich has one very impressive green area, the vast **Englischer Garten★** (English Garden), which cuts a wide swathe extending northwards from Prinzregentenstrasse all the way beyond the city limits. It is used all year round for strolling or jogging, and in summer, the generous lawns attract people in droves, to sunbathe, picnic, go riding, play drums or football, walk the dog, or even to practise martial arts such as Capoeira and Tai Ch'i. The **Eisbach** (Ice Stream) provides welcome relief on particularly hot days, and offers the challenge of trying to surf where the current forms a permanent curl (*see* p.111).

In the mid-18C, this entire area was an untamed landscape of bushes, trees and fields used for grazing and for the deer of the ducal house. In 1784, Duke Karl Theodor employed Benjamin Thompson, an American from Massachusetts who had fought for the English side in the War of

Bavaria suddenly meets Beijing – the Chinese Tower in the Englischer Garten.

Independence and then fled to Europe, to redesign the park. The great landscape architect Friedrich Ludwig von Sckell was also invited to draw up plans, and the Englischer Garten was born. A resemblance to Kew Gardens in London is by no means coincidental. Sckell designed the **Chinesischer Turm** (Chinese Tower) in 1790 in imitation of the Great Pagoda at Kew. It is perhaps the park's most famous landmark, and serves as a roof for a band. The **beer garden** is one of the most popular in Munich. In the 19C, servants and valets used to come here at the break of dawn on Sundays in summer to dance. The so-called **Kocherlball** (Cooks' Ball) was revived on the occasion of the Englischer Garten's 200th anniversary in 1989, and is now held every year on the third Sunday in July.

Among the park's many attractions are several statues, including one of Thompson (also known as Count von Rumford) and one of Sckell. Near the south entrance, there is a **Japanese Tea House** that was given to Bavaria during the Olympic Games in 1972. Tea ceremonies are held here from April to October.

Just south of the Chinese Tower stands Leo von Klenze's **Monopteros**, a little temple perched on top of an artificial mound that offers a wonderful view of the Munich skyline. Another very popular beer garden is the **Seehaus** (Lake House), on the banks of the Kleinhesseloher See to the north of the Chinese Tower. If business contacts prove hard to track down ('in a meeting') on a hot and sunny summer's day, go and have a look for them at the Seehaus or the Chinese Tower. After all, everyone in Munich meets there.

FURTHER AFIELD

Schloss Schleissheim★

The S1 leads north (15km/9 miles) to what was to be Munich's Versailles, **Schloss Schleissheim★**, commissioned by Elector Max II Emanuel from the Swiss architect Enrico Zuccalli in 1701. His plans had to be changed when the Elector was forced to flee the country and the resulting building turned out somewhat smaller than intended. Cosmas Damian Asam and François Cuvilliés the Elder were among the artists who worked on the magnificent decoration. In summer, the grand ceremonial room in Schleissheim is the venue of a delightful series of concerts.

The elegant façade of Schloss Schleissheim.

In the grounds are the **Altes Schloss** (Old Palace), which was built about a century

earlier for Elector Maximilian, and the Baroque folly, **Schloss Lustheim** (Lustheim Palace), also a masterpiece by Zuccalli, which Max Emanuel gave his first wife, Maria Antonia, as a wedding present.

Nymphenburg★★

The **Schlosskanal** (literally Castle Canal) provides an extraordinary view all the way to the front of **Nymphenburg Palace★** (6km/4 miles from the city centre), which was a present from Elector Ferdinand Maria to his wife Henriette Adelaide of Savoy. Construction began in 1664 under Agostino Barelli and continued under the Swiss architect Enrico Zuccalli. Throughout the 18C the palace was redesigned, refurbished and extended by a host of great artists, including the Cuvilliés and Johann Baptist

Experience a Bruegel snow scene first-hand when the Schlosskanal freezes up in winter.

Carved relief in a wall-niche, the Amalienburg.

Zimmermann, until it reached its current impressive size.

Twenty rooms in the main building are open to the public. The most breathtaking is the **Steinerner Saal** (Great Hall), which serves as the entrance. Its impressive size is enhanced by the wonderful light that glitters playfully on all the ornamentation. The other rooms in the two wings consist of antechambers, galleries and bedrooms, mostly in the French style. French Baroque predominates in the south wing. The famous **Gallery of Beauties★** contains 36 portraits commissioned by King Ludwig I, with the intention of immortalising some of the most beautiful women of his day (including Lola Montez, one of the king's mistresses, as well as a number of noblewomen). One of the bedchambers contains an unexpected surprise – a small cabinet containing a beautiful collection of Chinese lacquer work.

The **porcelain collection★** and **Museum Mensch und Natur** (Museum of Man and Nature) are located in the northern pavilions, while the **Marstallmuseum** (Coach Museum) in the south pavilions contains a collection of extraordinarily decorated coaches, intricate examples of the art of making harnesses, and paintings of the royal horses.

The park has a number of little treasures hidden away among the greenery, such as the **Badenburg**, a bathing 'castle' which once boasted a heated swimming pool, and the **Pagodenburg** (Pagoda Castle), which was Joseph Effner's answer to the taste for things Chinese that spread across Europe at the beginning of the 18C. The

The Steinerner Saal, Nymphenburg Palace, is a symphony of gold, white and pale green.

Amalienburg★★ is a little hunting lodge that was decorated by Cuvilliés the Elder, Zimmermann and Dietrich. It was built between 1734 and 1739 for Maria Amalia, the wife of Elector Karl Theodor, and represents one of the highlights of Rococo art in Germany. The **Palmenhaus** (Palm-Tree House) offers food and drink on a sunny terrace. To the north of the park are the splendid **Botanischer Garten★★** (Botanical Gardens). Stroll through the rhododendron walks, and marvel at the Alpine Garden by the Great Lake and the orchids and other tropical species in the glasshouses.

Dachau

An indelible reminder of Man's inhumanity to Man.

The pretty little town of Dachau (19km/12 miles north-west; on the S2 line) was the birthplace of the great architect Joseph Effner. He even built a charming Renaissance palace on the remains of a medieval castle; only the western wing remains, containing a ceremonial room with a coffered ceiling. However, the name Dachau is inevitably associated with the concentration camp which served as a 'model camp' for all others. It was the first to be opened and one of the last to be liberated. The death march of the last inmates has been memorialised by little statues in the various communities through which they passed (in Pasing, for example). Over 32 000 people died or were murdered here in very harsh conditions, and thousands more died in the 'outer camps' such as Kaufering and Allach, where they worked as slaves. The camp, a very searching and emotional experience, is open to visitors.

EXCURSIONS:
LUDWIG'S BAVARIAN CASTLES

Füssen★ provides and ideal base for
exploring the Bavarian castles of
Neuschwanstein, Linderhof and
Hohenschwangau, while the **Chiemsee★**
region is convenient for Herrenchiemsee.
*Füssen: Tourist information is available at the
Kurverwaltung, Kaiser Maximilian Platz 1,
87629 Füssen, ☎ (0 83 62) 70 77/ 8, Fax: (0 83
62) 3 91 81. They can help with accommodation,
which can be difficult to find in the summer
season.*
The **Chiemsee** *region has ample accommodation,
ranging from luxury hotels to simple and family-
oriented B&Bs. The boats to the island run all
year, but not at night. For more information:
Tourist Board of Upper Bavaria,
Pf 600320, D- 81203 Munich, ☎ (0 89) 82 92
18/0, Fax: (0 89) 82 92 18/28.*

Map of Bavaria

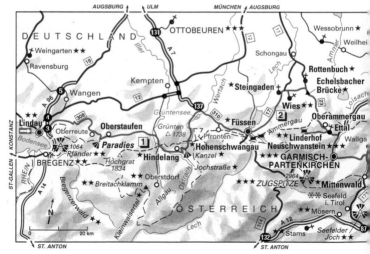

Wieskirche★★

If you are staying in Füssen, you may consider an excursion 26km (16 miles) north to **Wieskirche★★** (Church of the Flogged Saviour) in Steingaden. According to legend, Maria Lory, a peasant woman, found a representation of the Flogged Saviour in the attic of a local inn. It had been created in 1730 in Steingaden by monks for a Good Friday procession. Lory took the work to her home to revere it in private. In 1738 the Saviour shed tears, a genuine miracle that prompted the abbot of Steingaden to build a church to accommodate the flow of pilgrims. The yellow church rises out of the surrounding flower-covered fields as if it had always been there. Inside, the ceiling fresco representing the Flogged Christ is considered one of the finest masterpieces of Johann Baptist Zimmermann.

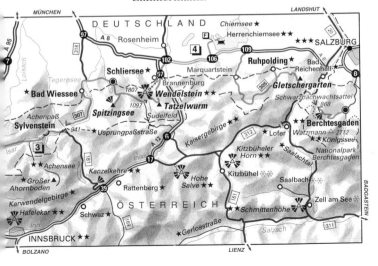

Schloss Neuschwanstein★★★

Ludwig II, who took the throne in 1864, grew up in his father's castle at Hohenschwangau, with the Alps on one side and the rich and harmonious tapestry of Bavaria's lakes and meadows on the other. The name Schwangau, a region named by the 'Swan Knights', suited him perfectly. The swan, his favourite animal, is a symbol of beauty and features prominently in Wagner's opera *Lohengrin*.

The castle of Neuschwanstein, eerily lit at night, seems as lonely and phantom-like as its builder, Ludwig II, the 'Mad King' of Bavaria.

It was in this setting that Ludwig II embarked upon his first project, the castle of **Neuschwanstein★★★**, a magical and theatrical creation in white that seems to grow straight out of a rocky crag. The Romanesque design was by Christian Jank, a stage designer who was not concerned with the physical implementation of his ideas. All rooms have been carefully furnished and decorated only with the finest crafts. The neo-Gothic wooden baldachin above Ludwig's bed alone took 14 woodcarvers more than four years to complete.

The two most breathtaking rooms are the Throne Room and the Singers' Hall. The **Throne Room** is Byzantine in inspiration, with a huge brass and gold-leaf chandelier shaped like a Byzantine crown. The floor, partially covered by a rug to protect it from the thousands of shuffling feet, is a vast mosaic of over 2 million tesserae depicting flora and fauna.

The **Singers' Hall** is an imitation of the 'Sängerlaube' in the Wartburg at Eisenach, where the Minnesänger once held their singing contest. Once again, the decoration borrows a great deal from the art of Byzantium, but the motifs are from Wagner's *Parcifal*. Christian Jank himself drew *Klingsor's Magic Garden*, covering the entire end of the room. The coffered painted pine ceiling was well designed for acoustics, and if you are lucky one of the more musical members of the tour party might sing a few notes as a test. It is still used for concerts because of both its atmosphere and excellent acoustics.

Wagner, whom Ludwig admired as an artist, friend and possibly father figure, also inspired other rooms in Neuschwanstein. In his bedchamber, the king had various episodes of *Tristan and Isolde* painted on the walls, in his study he could follow the progress of Tannhäuser, from his dallying with Venus to his humble pilgrimage to Rome. Even in the king's dressing room, the walls narrate the life of Minnesinger Walther von der Vogelweide.

Sadly, he lived there for only 170 days, and the castle was not fully completed before Ludwig's death. It was at Neuschwanstein that he received news of his dethronement, on 10 June 1886. He was found dead in Lake Starnberg three days later. Fortunately, the castle was not destroyed, as he had ordered it should be after his death, so visitors today can share in his fantasies and enjoy the castle.

Nestled in the wooded Bavarian hills, Schloss Hohenschwangau was home to the young Ludwig II.

Schloss Hohenschwangau★

A visit to **Hohenschwangau★** adds a further dimension to Neuschwanstein. Ludwig II spent the first 17 years of his life in this castle, which had been built by his father, Maximilian II.

The predominant style is Gothic, though some of the furnishings have a fairly solid, middle-class character about them, except for the lavish table setting in the banqueting hall. The frescoes all relate medieval events, the life and times of the Knights of the Schwangau, the story of the Duchess of Bouillon and various other legends. The artist was Moritz von Schwind (1804-71), a Viennese painter, whose style combined lyricism, realism and wonderful transparency.

Medieval English castle influences show in the crenellated roof and towers of Schloss Hohenschwangau.

*The romantic
fantasies of Ludwig
were encapsulated
in Schloss
Linderhof.*

Schloss Linderhof★★

Ludwig's great Bourbon namesakes Louis
XIV and Louis XV were the inspiration
behind **Linderhof★★**, a little jewel of a castle
set in a wooded narrow east-west valley
known as Graswang, to the east of Füssen. In
the entrance stands an equestrian statue of
Louis XIV (a replica of the one that once
stood on Place Vendôme, in Paris), behind
which glistens a great Sèvres vase. The
ceiling features a radiant golden stucco sun
bearing the Bourbon motto '*Nec pluribus
impar*' (equal to none).

  This overture is the prelude to a veritable
symphony of opulence: gilded stucco,
murals, delicate vignettes, putti, statuettes,
Meissen and crystal chandeliers, musical
instruments and luxurious divans. A high
point of this delightful and extravagant little
palace, and Ludwig's favourite room, is the
mirror room, decorated with over 90
Nymphenburg porcelain vases and vessels, a

*The exotic
extravaganza of the
Moorish 'kiosk',
Schloss Linderhof.*

glorious lapis-lazuli mantelpiece adorned with gilded brass and an extraordinary ivory chandelier. The landscaped **garden**★★ boasts the little **Chapel of St Anna** and an exotic Moorish '**kiosk**', which was originally built for the World Exhibition in Paris in 1867. The finest folly of all at Linderhof is the **Venusgrotte**, an artificial cavern decorated with stalagmites and stalactites and with an 'underground' lake at its centre. This was Ludwig's own private concert hall, where he could listen to Wagner's music and even, occasionally, take a swim. Technologically, the Venusgrotte had nothing mythological about it. Electricity was installed and BASF worked for two years to find the right blue colouring for the lighting, but it served to fulfil Ludwig's romantic fancies.

Schloss Herrenchiemsee★★

In 1873, Ludwig purchased Herrenwörth island in **Chiemsee**★, the province's largest lake. In 1878, work was begun on transforming Georg Dollmann's blueprints of **Herrenchiemsee**★★ into reality. The result was a series of reception rooms leading off from the top of a splendid staircase made from 16 different types of marble. From room to room, the decor becomes grander, increasingly opulent and complex, and even, at times, oppressive. The first antechamber contains a huge Boulle cupboard. The second chamber is an imitation of the oeil-de-boeuf room at Versailles. The bedchamber, the consulting cabinet and finally the extraordinary 98m- (320ft) long **Mirror Gallery** leave the viewer dazzled by all the intricate golden stucco work and huge crystal chandeliers.

Ludwig had his private quarters decorated

The dazzling Mirror Gallery, Schloss Herrenchiemsee.

in a slightly more modest style, with more blues, his favourite colour, to soften the harsh and relentless glint of gold.

Ludwig also had a 'bathroom' installed, appropriately adorned with balneological scenes, along with a dressing room in which he could see himself from all sides. At the time of his death, over 20 million marks had been spent on the building of the castle – Ludwig spent just one week there.

WEATHER

As far as climate is concerned, Southern Bavaria comes under both continental and the warmer, more humid, Atlantic influences. It is sunnier than many places in Germany, though at times, owing to strange climatic inversions in winter, Munich can be covered by a 'bell' of icy mist, while the rest of Bavaria is enjoying a heavenly sun bath. The close proximity to the Alps also accounts for the unpredictability of Munich's weather.

However, it does have four distinct seasons, without any extreme temperatures. Winter can be very cold at times, with lots of snow (bring properly insulated winter boots). Spring begins early, but has cold snaps well into May. Summers are warm, sunny and generally dry in 'good' years, with occasional thunder storms, but can be rainy and cold in 'bad' years. Autumn can be particularly beautiful, with warm Indian Summer days that end in chilly but clear nights. Be prepared for rain, though, and always plan for cooler weather. People like to meet in beer gardens, even early on in the season, braving cool evening breezes and the settling dew.

A word of warning: if you wake up one beautiful, sunny morning with a wrenching headache and have no intake of beer to blame for it, you may be one of the many people who are sensitive to the *Föhn*. This warm wind from the south has a strong effect on people. Moods at this time are subject to abrupt change, usually for the worse, headaches are frequent, people feel miserable.

CALENDAR OF EVENTS

January

Three Kings (6 January) is celebrated in Bavaria with children dressed up as Caspar, Melchior and Balthasar, walking about singing songs – for a Deutsch mark or two! *Fasching* (Carnival) begins in earnest, with celebrations, parties and balls.

February

Mardi Gras opens with the *Market Women's Dance* on Viktualienmarkt, followed by celebrations throughout the city. Lent begins on Ash Wednesday with fasting. The *CBR* holiday trade fair attracts thousands at the ICM fairgrounds.

March

Starkbierzet, the 'Strong Beer' season, begins around 19 March (St Joseph's): politicians and VIPs meet at the Nockherberg Paulaner Brewery to drink freshly tapped dark beer. The

International Crafts Fair IHM is held at the ICM, with every type of handicraft represented, from building to bakery.

April

The *Munich Biennale*, held in odd years, presents new music theatre. *Spring Festival* begins on the Theresienwiese, a kind of mini-Oktoberfest. The *Auer Maidult* on Mariahilfplatz begins around 1 May (and is repeated in summer and autumn, *see* below), with everything from cakes to junk and real antiques on sale.

May

Fronleichnam (Corpus Christi), on the second Thursday after Whitsun, begins at 8am with a religious service on Marienplatz, followed by a procession through the decorated streets. *BMW Open* Bavarian tennis championship. *Maypole* festivals are held around Bavaria. *Union Move*, the techno demonstration, is held on a Saturday afternoon on Leopoldstr., with techno celebrations focused on Kunstpark Ost.

June

On the second weekend in June is the city's *Foundation Festival*, with international celebrations and stands. *Tollwood*, an international festival of art, dance, theatre, circus and cuisine, is

Traditional Bavarian clock.

held in the Olympiapark. At the end of June/early July is the *International Film Festival*.

July

Munich's *Opera Festival* is held throughout the month, including ballet, concerts and recitals. *Art Open Air* presents performances on Königsplatz. The *Jakobidult* summer market is held on Mariahilfplatz (*see Auer Maidult* above).

August

The *Summer Festival* in the Olympiapark, with a fair and music ranging from classical to pop, on the Olympia Lake Theatron stage.

September

Oktoberfest begins on the penultimate weekend in September (*see* p.99). The *Compaq Grand Slam Cup Final* is held in the Olympic Hall.

October

The third market on Mariahilfplatz is held, the *Kirchweihdult*.

November

Six-day bicycle races are held in the Olympic Hall.

December

The beginning of Advent

signals the opening of the *Christkindl* markets throughout the city (especially Marienplatz, Rotkreuzplatz, Münchener Freiheit, Mariahilfplatz). The *Winter Tollwood* festival is held near Hacker Bridge, behind the main train station.

Oktoberfest celebrations.

ACCOMMODATION

Munich has a long history of welcoming visitors, tourists and business people alike, and there is no shortage of hotels and B&Bs in the city. Do be careful, however, if travelling during the high season in summer, around Oktoberfest, or during some of the big trade fairs (the IHM crafts show in March, for example). Prices do tend to fluctuate according to the time of year. The tourist information at the main train station or on Marienplatz can help find rooms on arrival, or you can call ahead ☎ **(089) 233 302 35/7**. Or try the German Hotel Reservations Service (**Allgemeine Deutsche Zimmer-reservierung** or ADZ) for all of Germany, Corneliusstr. 34, D-60325 Frankfurt, ☎ **(069) 74 07 67**.

If you are planning to stay longer in Munich, the **Mit-wohnzentralen** often have low-priced rooms available in private homes. You pay rent and a small commission to the agency. For details, contact City Mitwohnzentrale, Lämmerstr. 4 (near the station), ☎ **194 30**; or Mitwohnzentrale an der Uni, at the U-Bahn stop Universität (U3 or U6), ☎ **286 60 60**.

The Michelin *Red Guide Deutschland* lists accommoda-tion and restaurants in Munich and the other towns of Bavaria and Germany, for visitors who wish to make overnight stops or tour the surrounding area. It is updated annually.

The following accommodation suggestions have been grouped into three price categories: luxurious (DM 330 or above), moderate (DM 180-330) and economy (DM 190 or less). The prices are for a double room with bath and breakfast (generally), and refer to the top price. A brief section for young travellers follows.

Recommendations

Luxury Hotels
First and foremost in this category are the traditional hotels: the grand old **Bayerischer Hof** on Promenadenplatz (☎ 212 00); the **Kempinski Hotel Vier Jahreszeiten** on Maximilianstr. (☎ 212 50); the **Königshof** on Karlsplatz (☎ 55 13 60); the **Platzl Ringhotel** at Sparkassenstr. 10 (☎ 23 70 30), which was entirely restored in the 1990s; and on the right bank of the Isar, the **Prinzregent** at Ismaningerstr. 42 (☎ 41 60 50), with a somewhat weighty Bavarian style.

The hotel chains have also settled in town, at times with a broader pricing system. The **City Hilton** at Rosenheimerstr. 15 (☎ 480 40) stands right by the Gasteig, and is a comfortable walk into the centre of town. The **Marriott** is a modern building in the northern section of Schwabing, Berlinerstr. 93 (☎ 36 00 20), and the **Forum** overlooks Munich from its perch on Hochstr. in Haidhausen (☎ 480 30).

Moderate Hotels
The number of hotels in this category is endless, and includes most of the establishments within reach of the main train station. **An der Oper**, at Falkenturmstr. 10 (☎ 290 02 70), is a modern building which, as the name implies, is ideal for visitors coming to hear opera. The **Blattl** chain has two especially nicely located establishments in Munich – the **Parkhotel** im Lehel (Unsöldstr. 10, ☎ 21 10 50) and the **Altmünchen** in the Au (Mariahilfplatz 4, ☎ 54 84 40). The newly-renovated **Biederstein** on Biedersteinerstr., right by the Englischer Garten (U-6 Dietlindenstr., ☎ 39 50 72), is quiet, with excellent service. Located in a nice old townhouse on St-Paul-Str. opposite the eponymous church, is the **St Paul**, a few steps to the Theresienwiese (☎ 54 40 78

00). Another pleasant family-run business is the **Rotkreuzplatz**, on Rotkreuz-platz, a modern building but with the feeling of 'living' in Munich, especially since the breakfast room is in the neighbouring café.

Economy Hotels
A tall, narrow building on Viktualienmarkt, Heiliggeiststr. 6, is the home to **am Markt**, an experience considering the surrounding area (☎ 22 50 14). The **Ibis** chain has several hotels in Munich, including the **Münchener City** on Dachauer-str. (☎ 55 19 30), near the train station, offering modern comfort near the centre, at reasonable rates. The **Occam** is small but in a perfect setting in the middle of Schwabing (Occamstr. 7, ☎ 33 25 11). The **Nymphenburg**, a comfortable, modern hotel with a shady garden on grand old Nymphen-burgerstr. 141 (☎ 121 59 70), is worth a try, though prices go up to the moderate range as well.

Lodgings for Young People
The **hi** or **Haus International** (Elisabethstr. 87, ☎ 12 00 60) has over 540 beds, amenities such as a heated swimming pool, conference rooms, table-tennis rooms, etc., and is perfectly located on Hohen-

zollernplatz. Prices range from DM 110/day (single room with full board) to DM 40/day for a 5-bed room. The **DJH hostel** on Wendl-Dietrich-Str. 20, in Neuhausen (U1 Rotkreuzplatz), costs DM 25,50/day with breakfast. The age limit is 26 and you will need a membership card of the DJH: telephone the central office in Detmold at ☎ (05231) 741 10, or if in Munich contact the **Youth Information Centre** at Paul Heyse-Str. 22 (west of the train station), ☎ 51 41 06 60. The DJH hostel in beautiful Schwaneck Castle, outside Munich, in Pullach, costs between DM 20 and 24 and is an experience (S7 to Pullach) ☎ 793 06 44. In the west of Munich, near the Botanical Gardens, is **Das Zelt**, a huge campsite and recreational area with beer garden, bicycle rentals and so on, for young people. Information is available at the Youth Information Centre.

FOOD AND DRINK

Beer, naturally, is Bavaria's national beverage but, though many seem to try, no-one can actually live on beer alone, and therefore must at some point turn to more solid nourishment. Bavaria's gastronomic tradition may not be as fine and refined as the cuisine in other regions or countries, but it is tasty, filling, simple and, oddly enough, famous the world round for precisely those qualities. Of course in most restaurants the tendency is toward internationalism, and these days next to the standard Bavarian fare in more modern restaurants, you may well find such un-Bavarian dishes as Thai Tom Kha Gai soup, Bouillabaisse and a plate of roast beef. But why travel to Munich if that is your choice?

Bavarian cuisine stems from the more humble classes. Soups usually consist of a broth with something added, pancake strips (*Fritatensuppe*), fried dough bits (*Backerbsensuppe*) or a savoury liver dumpling (*Leberknödelsuppe*). Humble, too, is the pig that constitutes the mainstay in local kitchens. As a main course, you must try *Schweinsbraten mit Knödel*: pork roast with dumplings, washed down with beer. The roast should have a nice crispy crust

on it. A delicate variation of *Schweinsbraten* is *Spanferkel* (suckling pig). If you're very hungry, try the *Schweinshaxe*, pig hocks, which also comes with *Knödel*, but don't expect to walk around any museums afterwards. *Knödel*, by the way, is the Bavarian (and Bohemian) equivalent of pasta or rice. It consists of a mighty ball either of day-old bread (*Semmelknödel*) mixed with eggs and milk, or is made of grated potatoes (*Kartoffel* or *Erdäpfelknödel*).

Another inexpensive and tasty speciality is *Beuschl* or *saueres Lüngerl*, chopped calf's lung in a spicy sauce served with a *Semmelknödel*. Similar is *Rahmschwammerl*. It looks a little like *Beuschl* with its great Semmelknödel weighing down the plate, but consists of a saucy ragout of mushrooms (either fresh cepes or chanterels). Less exotic and always filling after a heavy day of sightseeing are *Knödelgröstl*, fried Knödel slices with eggs and sometimes diced bacon, or *Kasnockerl*, small dumplings with cheese, fried and served in a skillet. It is not truly Bavarian, but definitely Alpine and is found in every restaurant.

Among the more graceful dishes to appear on the Bavarian table are various recipes using trout (*Forelle*) from Bavaria's streams (either steamed, or *blau*, or simply fried), or the perch-like *Rencke* from Lake Starnberg, which is sometimes served smoked with freshly grated horseradish. Also served with horseradish is *Tafelspitz*, a tender fillet of beef boiled in vegetable broth. It's actually an Austrian import, but that fact is conveniently forgotten by genuine Munich patriots.

Bavarians do a fair amount of snacking, which comes under the general heading *Brotzeit*, literally bread-time. People on the fly visiting or taking a break from the office, will usually nip to the local butcher (*Metzger*) and grab a *Leberkäsesemmel*, a roll garnished with a slice of

Leberkäse (liver cheese), a meat loaf containing neither cheese nor liver. The *Fleischpflanzerl* is another *Brotzeit* option, a spicy hamburger that should be about half an inch thick at least!

Munichers also have their own form of tapas for beer. There is the *Radi*, for example, white radish sliced very thin and sprinkled with salt, a *Brezen* (pretzel) and occasionally slices of *Schmalzbrot*, dark bread with pork fat and crackling. *Obatzta*, which translates roughly as 'smeared', is a spread based on camembert, cream cheese, butter, onions, paprika and a shot of beer. For a slightly larger hunger there is *Tellersulz* (boiled pork and vegetables in

Café at the Müllersches Volksbad.

Beer

Beer in Bavaria, and especially in Munich, is more than just a thirst-quencher: it is a tradition, an industry, a pastime and a social event. Well over half of the 1 270 breweries in Germany are located in Bavaria, with seven huge operations in Munich doing terrific business. The sheer variety and subtlety of flavours, the thirst-quenching qualities that put any other drink to shame, and the modest price make beer not only a very popular drink but also a hot export item. It is also completely natural. Thanks to a law promulgated in Munich in 1487 by Albrecht IV the Wise, only water, hops and malt can be used to make beer. The Purity Law (*Reinheitsgebot*), is the world's oldest foodstuff regulation. As former German President, Richard von Weizsäcker, said: 'What a blessing it would be if the air were as clean as the beer!'

Beer comes in a great many variations – dark *Bocks*, light-coloured lagers (*Helles*), the special wheat-based *Weissbier*, cloudy organic brews, alcohol-

free or as shandy (*Radler*) and Coca-cola (*Russenmass*). Beer has its own calendar in Munich as well. The 'Fifth Season' begins in Lent, with the tapping of the dark 'Doppelbock' called Salvator, at the Paulanerkeller on the Nockherberg. This beer was originally brewed by the Pauline monks (hence the name) to celebrate the name day of the founder of the order. During the 'strong beer days' (*Starkbierzeit*), other brewers also produce their own special Doppelbock, giving it names that end in '-ator' (e.g. Operator).

When the first rays of sun start warming the air in spring, Munichers converge on their beer gardens. Under great, blooming chestnut trees, they indulge in beer and specialities such as cheese spread (*obatzda*), white radish (*radi*), huge pretzels, roast chicken, pork knuckle, spareribs and potato salad (almost always self-service). Time – and plenty of it – is the vital element for the beer garden experience. People from all walks of life sit at long tables and always find something or someone to talk about, often well into the night.

Finally, there is **Oktoberfest**, which began as a horse race held on the occasion of the marriage between the Bavarian Crown Prince Ludwig and Princess Theresa von Sachsen-Hildburghausen, on 12 October 1810. The race was repeated in 1811, and embellished with an agricultural fair. The meadow where it took place was named Theresienwiese, after the Princess, but is now referred to as the 'Wies'n'. This huge folk festival also means good business for the city and its brewers, who produce a special beer for the occasion.

On a Saturday in late September, after a variety of parades and ceremonies – and after weeks of setting up the huge beer hall tents, Ferris wheels, shooting galleries and roller-coasters – it is the duty of the Mayor of Munich to crack open the first barrel in front of an expectant crowd. After his cry of 'O'zapt is!', meaning 'It has been tapped,' the drinking, eating and fun and games can begin.

Oktoberfest revellers in beer tent.

aspic and pickles), cold pork roast, cheese and cold-cut platters hot or cold, sausage salad (*Wurstsalat*).

The most famous *Brotzeit* is the Munich *Weisswurst*, white veal sausages that are served in a bowl of hot water and are eaten with sweet mustard and pretzels as a rule. They are an integral part of *Frühschoppen*, a mid-morning snack with beer (it means early pint), which is especially popular after a long Sunday morning church service. Or instead of it. In order to blend in with the locals, do not cut your *Weisswurst* into little pieces to de-skin. The real Bavarian removes the entire skin with bold knife and fork movements and politely scrapes out the inside of the Wurst. After a few beers you might want to try the more plebeian *auszuzeln*, i.e., sucking out the insides of the *Weisswurst*. This method is fun, but will definitely brand you as a bumpkin.

Last but not least, Munich has a number of desserts to offer. Moving through town, you may want to stop at a bakery and eat an *Ausgezogene* (fried dough), fresh *Zwetschgendatschi* (plum cake), a *Rohrnudel* (a simple cake with a plum filling), or *Krapfen* (doughnut). Or you may choose to sit in a

Konditorei and enjoy a rich and creamy *Prinzregententorte*, a steaming *Dampfnudel* (a kind of boiled leavened dumpling stuffed with plum jam, originally from Austria, served with melted butter and poppyseeds), or apple rings fried in batter (*Apfelkücherl*). In restaurants the must to try is the calorie laden Bavarian Cream (*Bayerische Creme*), a vanilla-flavoured blancmange, or *Schupfnudel* (a kind of dumpling) with poppyseeds and sugar. Finally, *Reberdatschi* (fried potato pancakes with apple sauce) are usually found at open markets or at fairs.

Recommendations

Munich has a wide range of restaurants of all stamps. Check the *Michelin Red Guide Deutschland* as well. Here are a few suggestions, most of which serve traditional Bavarian cuisine.

Neuhausen

Löwengarten (*Volkartstr. 32, corner of Orffstr., U-Bahn Rotkreuzplatz* ☎ 16 13 73) Its small but diverse menu offers a small but excellent selection of Bavarian and international creations, in sparse surroundings.

Ysenegger (*Ysenburgstr. 3, U-Bahn Rotkreuzplatz* ☎ 16 27 91) A popular place with the younger crowd, serving typical Bavarian fare. Dark panelling, long tables, a little loud as the hour gets late.

Bachmaier (*Leonrodplatz, Tram 21 from the centre* ☎ **15 97 00 62**)
A 'Wirtshaus' in the old-fashioned style, with big tables, lots of dark wood panelling, and trophies galore hanging on the walls.

Old Town

Buxs (*Frauenstr. 9/Viktualienmarkt*) This vegetarian self-service restaurant is the place for a light lunch or a fully-fledged meal. Excellent salads and desserts (price by weight!). Buxs also has a branch at Amalienstr. 38.

Prinz Myschkin (*Hackenstr. 2, off Sendlingerstr.* ☎ **26 55 96**)
A vegetarian gourmet restaurant in very light and elegant setting, with a large non-smoking area.

Hundskugel (*Hotterstr. 18, off Sendlingerstr.* ☎ **26 42 72**)
Munich's oldest restaurant offers good cuisine at affordable prices in interesting, historic surroundings.

Pfälzer Weinprobierstube (*Residenz, opposite the Feldhernnhalle* ☎ **22 56 28**)
The name 'wine-tasting room' belies this large and popular place, with friendly service and its basic food at basic prices; big

light-coloured tables under a vaulted ceiling.

Dürnbräu (*Dürnbräugasse, off im Tal* ☎ **22 21 95**)
This restaurant has been operating for over 500 years; its secret to success is being simply Bavarian. The long table in the main dining room is unique, as is the tiny garden out back.

Maxvorstadt

Tresznejewski (*Theresienstr. 72, corner of Barerstr.*)
A typically up-and-coming place, with a long bar, many cocktails, somewhat hyperactive service, but a nice range of gastronomical specialities (and it stays open until 3am – a rarity).

Baal (*Kreittmayrstr. 26 corner Erzgiessereistr.* ☎ **18 70 38 36**)
Shelves full of books adorn one room, with dark panelling and a billiard table in the other room. Pagan divinities are the theme; a lively place off the beaten path, with a mixed crowd.

Atzinger (*Schellingstr. 9* ☎ **28 28 80**)
A place frequented by students who are not necessarily studying to be rich. No one complains about the food or the coffee.

Schwabing

Café Schwabing (*Kurfürstenplatz*)
A café for students and profes-

Künstlerhaus restaurant.

sionals. The decor could use a change, but the menu, while somewhat over students' budgets, is a good mix of nouvelle and bonne vieille cuisine.

Zum Spanferkel (*corner Franz-Joseph-Str./Kurfürstenstr.* ☎ 34 34 26)
A very homey place, simply decorated, serving good suckling pig (as the name suggests). Inexpensive menu with soup and an entrée every day.

Osterwaldgarten (*Keferstr. 12* ☎ 38 40 50 40)
A traditional restaurant and beer garden right on the Englischer Garten, with excellent food and a friendly atmosphere; prices are a little high ever since it was renovated. The garden is shaded by a huge old chestnut tree.

Bamberger Haus (*in Luitpold Park at Brunnerstr. 2; take the 27 tram to Karl-Theodor-Str. or the U2 or U3 to Scheidtplatz* ☎ 308 89 66) It's a little out of the way, but the historic Bamberger Haus, with its restaurant, brewery hall and delightful Italianate terrace set in Luitpold Park, is the place to celebrate.

Haidhausen
Hofbräukeller (*Wienerplatz* ☎ 459 92 50)
A big, old, traditional beer hall with a traditional beer garden attached, serving the same beer as the Hofbräuhaus but here the clientele is mainly Bavarian.

Kuchlverzeichnis (*Rosenheimer-str. 10* ☎ 48 17 49)
This somewhat above-average,

simply decorated restaurant is located in the shadow of the Gasteig and is a nice place to conclude an evening at the Philharmonie (reservations needed).

Zum Kloster (*Preysingstr. 77* ☎ 447 05 64)
A small, cosy establishment, with an alternative look and feel, tables outside in summer; essentially vegetarian with token meat dishes, and a view of the little old houses of Haidhausen.

No Mi Ya (*Wörthstr. 5* ☎ 448 40 95)
Worth mentioning for its exotic attempt at combining Japanese and Bavarian specialities – a novel idea that actually works.

Glockenbach

Faun (*Hans-Sachs-Str. 17* ☎ 26 37 98) The inhabitants of the Glockenbach quarter gather here for all occasions. Quite a wide range of dishes, from international to Bavarian.

Paulaner Bräuhaus (*Kapuzinerplatz* ☎ 53 03 31) A traditional old beer hall, very well refurbished, which brews its excellent beer on the premises. Big beer garden attached!

Cafés and Kneipen

Munich is densely packed with cafés or **Kneipen**, a cross between a coffee-house and a pub, several of which have been mentioned in the *Exploring* section of this book. Each tries to be different in this highly competitive market, but usually a certain social mix takes over and the establishment hardly ever changes. If you are about 45, were on the ecological barricades in the mid-1970s, you go to **Ruffini** in the Orff-Str., in Neuhausen. If you have a fairly well-paid job, you go to **Freiheit**, on Landshuter Allee (corner Leonrodstr.), which has good cocktails and is carefully dilapidated.

Schwabing is still the focus of the café and Kneipen scene. Fairly recent is **Kuletto's**, on Münchener Freiheit (corner Hesseloherstr.), which attracts a broad crowd, has good specials to eat and excellent coffee. The **Café Münchener Freiheit** opposite is a 'normal' place, with a wide selection of cakes and an extensive terrace. Down Leopoldstr., the cafés tend to lose their character entirely. The **Extrablatt**, on the corner of Georgenstr., has kept the same decor for ages (newspaper clippings) and is still an oldschool amusing place (it was launched by a local gossip columnist). Next to the State Library on Ludwigstr. is the **Café An Der Uni**, which looks like a warren of student digs, and has an amusing menu (e.g. the 'Mad Professor' sandwiches with salami and honey, or Nutella and ham).

The concentration of cafés in the student quarter increases considerably, with a nice mix ranging from the rough-cut, billiard-playing **Schelling-Salon** on Schellingstr. to the more standard **Vorstadt** at Türkenstr. 83, or the gathering places for the young and hip at **Puck** (Türkenstr. 33) and the tiny **Schneller** (Amalienstr. 59).

The classic old **Konditorei** offering cake, coffee and a dignified atmosphere can be found in the **Café Luitpold** (Briennerstr. 11) and **Kreutzkamm** (Maffeistr. 4) and the grand old **Dallmayr** on Dienerstr., which is also a traditional delicatessen. A real meeting place is the **Stadtcafé**, on St Jakobs-Platz, which boasts a good selection of international newspapers. In Haidhausen, the **Café Haidhausen** (Franziskanerstr. 4) is a general favourite; the **Preysing Garten** (Preysingerstr. 69) has an alternative flavour to it and a nice little garden; the **Atlas** (next to the Gasteig) seems filled with mobile telephones; and the **Grössenwahn** (Lothringerstr. 11) has a long tradition among artists and 'arteests'.

Beer Gardens

In Munich, you meet people you already know at cafés and Kneipen – at the beer gardens you might meet someone you *don't* know. Generally speaking, they all offer self-service Bavarian food, tables under big chestnut trees and lots of atmosphere. Here are a few suggestions:

Taxisgarten in Neuhausen (Taxisstr.)

Am Rosengarten (in Westpark, Westendstr. 305) in Westend/Laim

Hirschgarten (Neuhausen, off Wotanstr.)

Hirschau (Englischer Garten, north of the Mittlerer Ring)

Waldwirtschaft Grosshesselohe (in the south; take S7 or S27 to the Isartal Bahnof)

SHOPPING

Buying is something the people of Munich never seem to tire of, even in the face of depleted bank accounts. 'Man gönnt sich ja sonst nichts,' is a frequently heard expression, meaning 'You don't treat yourself often.' When the summer and winter sales are announced, the pedestrian shopping zones become so crowded you can hardly move, and there is a wealth of shops in Munich to choose from, so the question remains: what to buy?

Clothing

Every international designer is represented in town, but their wares are all limp-wristed when compared to *Tracht*, Bavaria's own national costumes, which – joking aside – has developed into quite a special fashion. Shops such as **Loden-Frey** (*Maffeistr.*) and **Wallach's** (*Residenzstr.*) have some very fine traditional costumes with chic variations. The prices are high but the quality is beyond reproach. Wallach's also sells original Bavarian arts and crafts, notably pottery with a blue and white design recalling the Bavarian flag. **Ludwig Beck am Rathaus Eck**, at the eastern corner of Marienplatz, has expanded considerably over the years and now includes a wide range of cloth, cosmetics, CDs and all sorts of clothing and finery. Two other traditional stores are nearby: **August**

The pedestrian zone.

Strauss (*Heiliggeiststr. 2*) and the tiny kiosk-like **Lederhosen Wagner** that is attached like a barnacle to the Heiliggeist Church on the im Tal side. Wagner also sells such items as traditional rucksacks. On the other side of the pedestrian zone in Herzogspitalstr. is **Leder-Moser**, who sell everything relating to *Tracht*.

Try browsing the student quarter (Schellingstr., Amalienstr., Theresienstr., Türkenstr., etc.) for more outrageous clothing in some of the second-hand shops. You might run across 1970s leather jackets, coats from the 1950s, genuine old linen peasant shirts, and accessories in all shapes and sizes from the past 100 years. **Holareidulijö** (*Schellingstr. 81*) specialises in old *Tracht*. In Schwabing, you might try **Karola's** in the Haimhauserstr.

One man's crusade against the killing of tigers has resulted in the very special **Tiger Store** (*Lilienstr. 7, across Ludwig Bridge*), where every piece of clothing, from shirts to lingerie, is in tiger print.

Food

Dallmayr's is Munich's grand old delicatessen, where you can find a wide range of teas, coffees, liquors and other exotica, either to take home or buy for your hosts. The **Spanisches Fruchthaus**, on Sendlingerstr., specialises in dried fruits of all kinds, and has a beautiful display to boot. **Elly Seidl Pralinenspezialitäten** at Kosttor 2 and Maffeistr. 1, is the place to satisfy a sweet tooth, or try the **Confiserie Leyssiefer** at Kaufingerstr. 9 (in the Asam passage), one of Munich's top addresses for fine chocolates. On Westenriederstr., you will find the **Tölzer Kas Laden**, a small cheese shop specialising in Upper Bavarian products. For a wide range of local foodstuffs, follow the locals to Munich's main food market, **Viktualienmarkt** (near Marienplatz), held Monday to Saturday.

Other Specialities

Popular souvenirs include beer tankards, traditional Bavarian costumes and costumed dolls, wood carvings, pewter ware and waxworks. **Nymphenburg porcelain** is popular with collectors, and while several shops around town do sell it, the best place is the outlet of the factory itself in the northern pavilions of Nymphenburg Palace. An interesting shop in Sendlingerstr., right next to the Asam Church, is the **rope-maker Kienmoser**, who sells ropes and threads of all kinds and various other

Beer tankards.

handicraft items. In the same vein is **Johanna Daimer Filze aller Art**, a tiny shop in the Neues Rathaus arcades on Dienerstr., which has every possible kind of felt you can imagine, and for every possible use. The **Papierladen**, at Schellingstr. 71, specialises in paper of all kinds and book-binding materials, while **Kunst und Spiel** at Leopoldstr. 48 has beautiful toys.

Markets

Trödel in German means junk, but a *Trödelladen* (junkstore) does not necessarily mean low prices anymore. All along **Westenriederstr.**, between Isartor and Viktualienmarkt, you can find antique shops that are dirty and dusty, but not cheap.

There are **flea markets** as well, held all around the city at various intervals, though the biggest and most regular one is held every week from Thursday to Saturday near the bus station on Arnulfstr. It's a genuine junk market, with only a few 'specialists' and hence lots of haggling. Otherwise, keep an eye out for the word *Flohmarkt*, or ask the tourist office for the dates of the market at Neusserstr. 21 in the north of Munich, or the market at the **Riem fairgrounds** (*Messegelände*).

Special markets and small trade fairs are sometimes held in the big beer halls, the **Paulaner** on Nockherberg, for example, or at the **Löwenbräu** hall at Stiglmaier Platz.

ENTERTAINMENT AND NIGHTLIFE

Munich has so many concert halls and venues for events that tickets are seldom sold out (for classical events). Besides the **National-Theater** (opera), there is a wide variety of musical events ranging from symphonic to solo, held in the **Philharmonie** (symphonic) of the Gasteig, at the beautiful **Staatliches Theater am Gärtnerplatz** (opera and operetta) and **Prinzregententheater** (operetta), and the **Cuvilliés-Theater** (spoken theatre), **Herkules-Saal**, **Max-Joseph-Saal** and **Residenztheater** (the last four in the Residenz). There

are dozens of other halls and venues, ranging from the **Olympic Hall**, used for big pop concerts, and the musical **Deutsches Theater** (*Schwanthalerstr. 13*) at one extreme, to a single room venue in **Café Ruffini** (*Orffstr. 22*).

Tickets: For the big events, it is best to book ahead through a travel agent or contact the Munich tourist office. Once in Munich, your hotel reception should be able to arrange tickets for you quite simply. There are several ticket agencies in the city:
München Ticket GmbH (☎ 54 81 81 81)
Tick Tick Tickets (in the

The intimate Cuvilliés-Theater, in the Residenz.

Karstadt at Neuhauserstr. 18, in the pedestrian zone ☎ **29 02 54 99**) for music, shows and sports events

Special Concerts at Saturn-Hansa (Schwanthalerstr. 115, ☎ **50 60 84**)

The Hertie at Münchener Freiheit (☎ **33 66 59**).

Munich's best programme magazine is the fortnightly *München IN*, which is full of useful information, addresses, telephone numbers and ads. It lists events day-by-day in a fairly clear manner, and even if your German is poor you can make out the words *Kino* for film, *Klassik* for classical and *Fernsehen* for television. The other headings are in English. Under the heading Kino, the abbreviation OmU (or OoU) means original language with (or without) subtitles. *Munich Found*, an English-language monthly, not only has articles on Munich but also includes a good selection of events and services for English-speakers.

The night scene in Munich is fairly varied. There are Irish pubs that offer good folk music, such as the **Shamrock** (*Trautenwolfstrasse. 6*), or fine jazz at the famous **Kaffee Giesing** (*Bergstr. 6*), once owned by singer-songwriter Konstantin Wecker. The **Nachtcafé** on Maximilianplatz also has jazz, but is more for the night-hawk scene. The **Oklahoma** (*Schäftlarnstr. 156*) offers Western style ambience and occasional country recitals, while at the **Vollmond** ('full moon', *Schleissheimerstr. 82*) you won't be blamed for thinking that the Age of Aquarius is upon us. The choice in this smaller, quasi-café scene really is endless and rich in Munich.

There are a number of bigger venues, of course, notably **Kunstpark Ost**, behind the Ostbahnhof (eastern train station), where the house, techno, grunge, hiphop and the rest of the pierced-tattooed-shaven scene meet and shake into all hours of the night. The halls are large, the furnishings are appropriately run down. A similar scene is developing around the **Millennium** and **Alabama Hall** on Domagkstr., in a dingy area of northern Schwabing, where some army barracks once stood. At Landsbergerstr. 185 is another dilapidated place called **Nachtwerk**, an old warehouse where anything goes, music-wise, it seems. The **Feierwerk** (*Hansastr. 39*) is smaller and more intimate. Live music and a generally relaxed young scene can be found at the **Backstage**, on the Neuhausen side of the Donnersberger Bridge.

Also a favourite, night and

day, are the events (jazz, funk, soul) held in the **Schlachthof**, the slaughterhouse (*Zenettistr. 9*), where the crowd tends to be a little older. The **Muffathalle**, at the Ludwig Bridge, offers a wide range of music and dance in a very enjoyable atmosphere, with anything from readings to dance theatre, from rap or ethno to world music.

Some of the places mentioned above have good dancing facilities, of course, but there are others, such as the **Park-Café** at the end of Meiserstr. in Maxvorstadt, **Crash** at Ainmillerstr. 10, or the **Liberty** at Rosenheimerstr. 30, the latter specialising in 1960s and 1970s music. Students tend to gather at the **Oly Disco** in the former Olympic village (*Helene-Mayer-Ring 9*), because entrance is cheap and the programme changes daily. The **Pulverturm**, out at Schleissheimerstr. 393 (U2 Am Hart), is often used for parties, but like the Backstage it has a nice beer garden outside for the summer and a chilling out tent for the winter. Finally, mention should be made of the **P1**, a somewhat pretentious place guarded by bouncers, in the rear of the Haus der Kunst, right on the Englischer Garten. Taken with humour, it's a very amusing place to be. If you get in …

SPORT

Sport and recreation are naturally high on Munich's agenda. What better way to explore the city and to get some exercise at the same time than by **bicycle**? Cyclists are well catered for, and the city boasts over 1 100km (684 miles) of bike paths. For a fare, you can take the bike on the S-Bahn (not in rush hour!) and leave the city for a day.

Swimming, too, is a widespread sport in Munich. Besides the Alpine lakes nearby, there are smaller ones in the immediate vicinity of the city (Langwiedersee, Feringasee, Feldmochinger See) and a number of outdoor and indoor pools in every corner of town: Dantebad and Westbad in the west, the Olympic pool in the north, the beautiful Müllerische Volksbad in the centre, to name but a few. The city baths are usually equipped with extensive and luxurious sauna and steambath facilities. **Watersports** and **boating** are catered for too. The Isar is a challenge for canoers and even rafters and surfboarders, while windsurfers and sailors can try their hand on the big lakes in the south.

In addition to the Olympic swimming pool, the old Olympic halls are still in use, and the **ice-skating** rink has been extended to include a

The Eisbach (Ice Stream) in the Englischer Garten offers the challenge of surfing where the current forms a permanent curl.

fully-fledged **inline-skating** rink.

Munich hosts two tennis tournaments, so it naturally has quite a few **tennis** courts. The **Sport Scheck** shop in Sendlingerstr. operates several courts in the Englischer Garten, the city power company has a few courts in Nymphenburg, and there is a club in Luitpoldpark.

However, it's the Alps that provide the major sporting playground of Munich. This major world city is just an hour's drive away from some of the finest **skiing** and **snow-boarding** in Europe. And indeed, almost every weekend from the first snow until April there are long traffic jams at the end of the A95 Autobahn to Garmisch-Partenkirchen, which nestles in the shadow of the 2 964m (8 322ft) Zugspitze. Religiously, the people of Munich enjoy their snow, be it that in **Garmisch**, **Mittenwald**, or in the other resorts that line the Alps – **Lenggries**, **Miesbach**, **Schliersee**, **Bayerischzell** and so on. If the snow is too wet or insufficient, they just drive another hour or so into Tyrol. Skiing can be easily done as a day-trip, but if you have the choice, try for a weekday.

It's little wonder Bavaria has become the focus of Germany's tourist industry, for in summer those very same Alps are the haunt of hikers, bikers, paragliders and mountain climbers.

THE BASICS

Before You Go

A valid passport (UK citizens) or a personal identity card (for EU residents) is sufficient for entry into Germany. Nationals from Australia, Canada, New Zealand and the USA may travel within Germany for up to three months without a visa, providing they hold a valid passport. No vaccinations are necessary.

Getting There

By air: Flughafen Franz Josef Strauss international airport (☎ (089) 97 52 13 13) is the main point of arrival and departure in Munich, some 30km (18.4 miles) north of the city centre. There are numerous direct flights from the UK and USA to Munich, with most of the main airlines represented. For information concerning **Lufthansa** (Germany's national airline) ☎ (089) 97 525 44.

By car: Travellers with EU driving licences may drive for up to a year in Germany. When driving from the UK, the best route to Munich is through Belgium to Köln (Cologne) and then down the A3. After Würzburg take the A7 towards Ulm and then the A8 to Munich, arriving at the Mittlerer Ring (Middle Ring Road) to the north-west of the city.

Travelling by car in Germany is also possible using the Mitfahrzentralen (car pools), of which there are several in Munich: Lämmerstr. 4 (near the main train station), ☎ 1 94 40; Amalienstr. 87, ☎ 1 94 44.

By coach: Munich has good coach connections to the rest of Europe. The bus station is located behind the main rail station (Hauptbahnhof). The Internationaler Busverkehr Deutsche Touring Reisebüro GmbH, in the north part of the rail station, has information on coach travel ☎ 545 87 00.

By rail: The journey time from Calais or Ostend to Munich is around 18 hours. The **Haupt-bahnhof** is Munich's main national and international rail station, has good connections with most major European cities, and is the major intersection for public trans-portation within the city. Travel information is available from 6am to 11pm daily, ☎ 01805 99 66 33 (*not* toll-free!). For reser-vations: ☎ (089) 13 08 23 33. In the UK, call German Rail telesales on ☎ (020) 8390 8833. When purchasing a ticket in Germany, be aware that you often have to pay an additional fee (for Inter-City trains, or the ICExpress trains, for example). Ask for details of weekend and family specials.

Note that some trains arrive at and depart from the **Ostbahnhof** (east train station), especially those to and from Austria and points south and east.

Arriving/departing

The best way to get into town from Franz Josef Strauss airport is by **S-Bahn 1 or 8**. The first S-Bahn leaves at around 4.06am, after which trains run every 20 minutes, with the last train at around 1.06am. The journey time is about 40 minutes, and the cost depends on which ticket you purchase (*see* Transport).

Buses leave from the airport into town every 20 minutes, between 7.55am and 8.55pm. The journey time is about 45 minutes, and tickets cost DM 15 (adult), DM 5 (child). There is a discount for return tickets.

The first S-Bahn train leaves the city centre for the airport at 3:15am and then every 20 minutes until 0.35am. Buses leave the Arnulfstrasse entrance of the main rail station, beginning at 6.50am and running every 20 minutes until 7.50pm. You can pick it up 10 minutes later at the corner of Isarring and Ungererstrasse (near the Marriott Hotel) in north Schwabing.

Paddle steamer on the Chiemsee.

Accidents and breakdowns

The ADAC is Germany's main automobile club and has mutual agreements with foreign clubs. For general information ☎ 01805 10 11 12; for the breakdown service ☎ 0180 222 22 22. In the event of a breakdown on the motorway, follow the little arrows on the guard-rail to the nearest emergency telephone.

If driving a rental car, call the firm in case of breakdown or accident.

Banks

Banks are usually open from 8.30am-12.30/1pm and 2.30pm-4pm (5.30/6pm on Thursday, and some are open until 6pm on other days as well). Generally, banks are closed at weekends. ATMs are very widespread, and most allow you to withdraw money on credit cards.

Bicycles

Using a bicycle is the best way of moving quickly and effi-ciently around Munich, especially since traffic is heavy and parking spaces rare. Ride your bike in the same direction as other road traffic and stick to the path; make sure you have lights for cycling at night; do not jump red traffic lights; be extra careful when crossing streets or garage exits. Like many city motorists, Munich drivers are often inconsiderate to cyclists, so care is needed. A new law allows cyclists to ride the wrong way down *some* one-way streets – a signpost indicates which ones. You can lose your driving licence if cycling under the influence of alcohol.

Several companies in Munich offer good and inex-pensive cycle tours, which include cycle hire:
Mike's Bike Tours,
☎ 651 42 75;
Spurwechsel,
☎ 69 37 00 02.
Several places in Munich rent out bicycles, including **Radius Touristik** in the main rail

station (from mid-April to mid October), ☎ 59 61 13.
See also **Transport**

Camping

Full details of campsites in Germany can be obtained from the **Deutscher Camping Club (DCC)**, Mandelstr. 28, D-80802 Munich ☎ 089 380 14 20 Fax 089 33 47 37. For 'Das Zelt' camping area for young people, see Accommodation, p.95. To the south of Munich is Thalkirchen campsite (Zentral-ländestr. 49, U3 Thalkirchen, and take the 57 bus, ☎ 723 17 07). There is a campsite at Eschenriederstr. 119 (where winter camping is also allowed on request), located at the Langwiedersee exit near the end of the A8 Autobahn from Augsburg, ☎ 864 15 66. There is another at Lochhausener-Str. 59, also near the end of the A8 Autobahn, ☎ 811 22 35.

Car Hire

All big international car hire agencies are represented in the city and at the airport. You should make sure you have full insurance cover, especially if you are unfamiliar with the rather brash driving style prevalent in Munich. Look for special weekend or package deals. The minimum age limit for hiring a car is 21, but some companies will not hire out to drivers younger than 23 or even 25.

Children

Munich is a child-friendly place, where young visitors are readily accommodated. This relaxed attitude manifests itself in restaurants, where 'our smaller guests' always have their own options on the menu. Children's beds, booster car seats and other useful equipment can be rented from *Littlebits*, Herren-str. 15, in the centre of Munich, ☎ 29 16 36 05. The **Kinder InfoLaden** at Albrecht-str. 37 provides information on programmes and other events for children (Tue-Fri 1pm-5pm).

There is plenty to keep children amused in Munich. The city has numerous swimming pools, both indoor and outdoor. The **Cosimabad** has a wave pool and the **Westbad** boasts a big slide. There are little playgrounds all over town (481 in all).

The **Tierpark Hellabrunn** has a section where children can stroke some of the animals, and offers rides on camels and even on an elephant. Munich also has its own circus, the **Zirkus Krone**, Marsstr. 43, S-Bahn Hacker-

brücke (west of the train station), ☎ **55 81 66**. There are two very fine puppet theatres in town: the **Marionetten-Theater**, Blumenstr. 29a, near Sendlinger Tor (☎ **26 57 12**), and Otto **Bille's Marionetten-bühne**, Breiteranger 15 (U1/U2 Frauenhoferstr).
Schauburg: Das Theater der Jugend on Elisabethplatz, in Schwabing, is famous in Germany (☎ **23 72 13 65**).

The **Deutsches Museum**, where science and technology can be experienced first hand, is the kind of place enjoyed by children of all ages.

Munich also has numerous **festivals** (the Spring Festival and even Oktoberfest), with roller-coaster rides and other hair-raising entertainment. The older, cooler kids will no doubt take to the roller-blading rink in the Olympiapark. A tour of the **Bavaria Film Studios** is a new and exciting event for the young and the young at heart, ☎ **64 99 23 04**.

Clothing

In summer, make sure you have something warm with you for cool evenings. Although not a particularly rainy place, Munich can have spells of wet weather, even in summer. Winter can be very cold at times, with lots of snow, so you will need warm clothing, warm socks and properly insulated boots. Spring begins early, but has cold snaps into May, so you should always provide for cooler weather. If you are planning to cycle a lot, you will need suitable rain-proof clothing.

The Germans still dress up smartly to go to the opera or theatre; visitors can get away without wearing evening dress, but jeans are definitely frowned upon.

Consulates

Australia and New Zealand have no representation in Munich, but can be contacted in Berlin and Bonn respectively.
Australia ☎ **(030) 880 0880**
New Zealand ☎ **(0228) 228 070**
British Consulate General Bürckleinstr. 10, ☎ **21 10 9 0**
Canadian Consulate General im Tal 29, ☎ **22 26 61**
US Consulate General Königinstr. 5, ☎ **28 88 0**

Crime

Munich is a safe city, by any standards, but you should nonetheless take basic precautions, such as locking up your car and closing the windows properly, avoid leaving valuables on show, keep your wallet in a safe place and do not brandish cash about. The area around Theresienwiese can become a little rough during the Oktoberfest, so do not let yourself be provoked. Play it safe in unfrequented areas and in tunnels or subways. Parking garages often have special spaces reserved for women that are under watch. Finally, in an emergency ☎ 110.

Customs and Entry Regulations

There is no limit to what can be brought into Germany from EU countries, provided it is for personal consumption. When in doubt, call your nearest German embassy. American citizens returning to the USA can file for a return on the Value Added Tax (Mehrwertsteuer). Ask for the form and a receipt when purchasing taxable goods (German VAT is currently 16%).

Disabled Visitors

Services for the disabled in public places are improving in Munich. The *Michelin Red Guide Deutschland* indicates which hotels have facilities for the disabled. In Britain, RADAR, at 12 City Forum, 250 City Road, London EC1V 8AF ☎ (020) 7250 3222, publishes fact sheets, as well as an annual guide to facilities and suitable accommodation overseas.

The Munich Tourist Office can also provide assistance

Decorative sign.

☎ **233 03 00**. For electronic travel information, ☎ **21 03 32 29**. A culture guide for the disabled is available at Ce Be eF, Knorrstr. 25, D-80807 Munich ☎ **356 88 08**. Public transport information for the disabled is available from the MVV, Thierschstr. 2, D-80538 Munich ☎ **21 03 30**.

Driving

Using a car in Munich is little more than a waste of precious time, considering the manageable size of the city, the lack of parking space in most central areas and the density of the public transport network. However, you may wish to use a car for excursions from the city.

UK citizens need a national driving licence and US citizens an international driving licence. Your vehicle must be properly insured (a green card is recommended) and a nationality plate is required. If driving a British car, dip the right beam or use tape to alter the angle of your headlight glare. Remember, in Germany you drive on the right.

The law requires you to carry in your car a warning triangle, a first aid kit and rubber gloves. You should also carry a reserve fuel canister. Seat belts must be worn in the

The Seehaus beer garden on the banks of the Kleinhesseloher See, in the Englischer Garten.

front and rear seats. Children up to 4 years of age must have a special seat; those up to 12 years of age or under 1.5m in height must have a booster cushion. Children under 12 are not allowed in the front seat. The blood alcohol limit for drivers is 0.5ml/g, although if there is an accident, insurance companies may not honour their commitment if the insured party had any alcohol at all in their blood. Motorways are toll free.

Note: US drivers unfamiliar with Germany may have trouble adjusting to the unwritten rules of the road. Driving in Germany is comparatively aggressive and uptight. On the Autobahn, avoid 'hogging' the fast lane or even the middle lane. If you are slow, your place is in the right-hand lane. Get used to having powerful cars riding your rear bumper and flashing you, even if you are passing a lorry or a slower driver.

Speed limits are as follows:
Maximum in built-up areas:
50kph/31mph
(in some cases 30kph/19mph)
Maximum outside built-up areas: 100kph/62mph
Recommended maximum motorway speed is 130kph/81mph
Cars pulling trailers (including caravans) are limited to a maximum of 80kph/50mph on roads and motorways.

Electric Current

The voltage in Germany is 220V. Sockets are of the two-pin variety. American appliances will require a transformer.

Emergencies

Police ☎ 110
Fire brigade and ambulance service ☎ 112
Medical emergency ☎ 55 17 71
Pharmacy emergency service ☎ 59 44 75
Dental emergency ☎ 723 30 93
Paediatric emergency ☎ 55 86 61

Etiquette

There are a few common courtesies that should be observed. On entering a shop or even a smaller inn, say *Grüss Gott* (good day) and on leaving say *Auf Wiedersehen* (good bye) or *Auf Wiederschaun* (which is more southern). It is courteous to shake hands when you greet someone. Do not jump the lights at pedestrian crossings or jaywalk (you can be fined for it), and avoid walking on the bicycle strip marked out on many sidewalks. Finally, remember being punctual is considered a positive virtue!

Health

Comprehensive travel insurance should be purchased before travelling, and in the event of illness keep all receipts carefully. UK nationals should take along Form E111 which entitles the holder to free emergency treatment for an accident or illness in EU countries (forms are available from post offices in the UK). In exchange for this form, the German Health Insurance Service (AOK, with offices everywhere) will give you a form entitling you to free health care. Munich has very high standards of health care.

Language

English is spoken quite frequently in Munich, especially by the younger generation. A few words of German are always appreciated. Do not worry if you cannot understand people in Bavaria well: the local dialect is quite strong and the words used are often

Yes/No / Ja/Nein

Please / Bitte

Thank you (very much) / Danke (sehr)

Good morning / Guten Morgen

Good day/hello / Grüss Gott

Goodbye / Auf Wiedersehen (fam. *Pfüati*)

Good evening / Guten Abend

Menu / Die Speisekarte

Water / Das Wasser

Beer / Das Bier

Wine / Der Wein

How much does it cost? / Wieviel kostet es?

The bill, please / Die Rechnung bitte

Do you speak English? / Sprechen Sie Englisch?

Where is …? / Wo ist …?

Left/Right / Links/Rechts

I don't understand / Ich verstehe nicht

I'm sorry / Es tut mir leid

Excuse me / Entschuldigung

I would like … / Ich möchte …

different from standard German.

Lost Property
City lost property office: Fundstelle der Stadtverwaltung, Oeztaler Str. 17 ☎ 233 00 (Mon-Fri 8.30am-noon).

German Railways lost property office: Fundstellen der Deutschen Bahn AG, Hauptbahnhof (main rail station) by track No 26 ☎ 13 08 58 59 (Mon-Fri 8am-noon, Tue 2pm-6pm); in Ostbahnhof (east rail station), counter No 8 ☎ 13 08 44 09 (Mon-Fri 8am-6pm, Wed. until 5pm only).

Airport lost property office: ☎ 975 213 70.

Maps and Guidebooks
The *Michelin Red Guide Deutschland* contains detailed information on hotels and restaurants throughout Germany, with maps of towns. The *Michelin Green Guide Germany* contains background information on the city and descriptions of the main attractions in the city. The Michelin road map **No 420** will assist you in planning your route if driving to Munich or making excursions from the city.

Money
The Euro now the official common currency between 11 countries, including Germany, but the Deutsche Mark is still legal tender. DM 1 is divided into 100 Pfennig. Bank notes come in denominations of 5 (very rare), 10, 20, 50, 100, 200, 500 and 1000 DM; coins come in 1, 2 and 5 DM, and 1, 2, 5, 10 and 50 Pfennig. There is no limit to the amount of Deutsche Marks or any other foreign currency that may be taken into or out of Germany.

The use of credit cards is common, especially in hotels, restaurants, department stores and at petrol stations. EU cards are also used very frequently for direct cash payments. Travellers' cheques in US Dollars and major European currencies are accepted, although DM travellers' cheques are preferred. *See also* **Customs**

Newspapers
Munich has an English-language magazine called *Munich Found*, which has supplied news of the city for over 12 years, including travel features, cultural items, interviews and so on, with an excellent listings section. It is available at some news stands and in hotels. For international news, the *International Herald Tribune* is on sale at most major news stands. It provides a concise look at polit-

ical and economic news and quotes the stock market. Most English-language newspapers (including the occasional New York *Times*) can be found at the news shop in the main rail station and the east rail station.

Opening Hours

Shops: Basic opening hours are 9am-6.30pm Monday to Friday. Some shops choose to stay open until 8pm. Opening hours on Saturday are usually 9am-1pm, but sometimes until 4pm or 5pm. Some bakers and florists open on Sunday mornings.

Museums and Galleries: These are, by and large, open from 10am-6pm, though some have extended opening hours on certain evenings (e.g. the Alte Pinakothek on Tuesdays). Most museums are closed on Mondays, but open on Sundays. The small museums, such as the one in Haidhausen, are open only sporadically (and then usually at weekends).

Chemists: *Apotheken* normally stay open until 6.30pm on weekdays and 1pm on Saturdays. The word *Bere-itschaftsdienst* means you can ring in an emergency, or it gives you the address of the nearest chemist that can process a prescription or sell

aspirin. *See also* **Banks**, **Post Offices**, **Emergencies**

Photography

Using a flash is not allowed in museums. Always ask before photographing to avoid problems (sometimes there are copyright issues involved). Excellent postcards and slides are available in most large museums.

Tip: Munich is flat, so photo-graphing it from above is perfectly possible. Try the Tele-vision Tower in the Olympiapark, the Olympia 'mountain', the tower of St Peter's church or the south tower of the Frauenkirche.

Post Offices

Post offices in Munich are usually open from around 8am-6pm on weekdays and 8am-noon on Saturdays, with the odd variation. The post office at Bahnhofplatz 1, opposite the railway station, stays open longer in the evening (until 8pm) and at weekends (until 4pm on Saturday and 3pm on Sunday).

Public Holidays

Bavaria, being profoundly steeped in Roman Catholicism, has quite a few holidays, espe-cially around spring.
New Year's Day: 1 January

Epiphany: 6 January
Good Friday to Easter Monday
May Day: 1 May
Ascension
Whitsuntide
Corpus Christi Day
Assumption of the Blessed
   Virgin Mary: 15 August
German Unification Day:
   3 October
All Saints' Day: 1 November
Christmas Day: 25 December
Boxing Day: 26 December

Telephones

Long-distance and local calls can be made from all post offices and public call boxes. The number of coin-operated public telephones has been decreasing, in favour of card-operated telephones. Post offices, news kiosks and even petrol stations sell telephone cards for DM 12 or DM 50. Also increasing is the number of credit card operated phones, which are convenient but usually on the expensive side. Calling from hotels is still very expensive, even though prices for telephone services generally have dropped drastically in the past few years since the market was deregulated. If you are planning to make many calls, it may be worth purchasing a pre-paid card or something similar in any phone shop.

To call Germany from abroad, dial **00 49** followed by the town prefix without the preceding 0 and then the number. To call another town within Germany dial the prefix with the zero. To dial a number within the same locality, drop the prefix altogether.
Munich's prefix is **089**
Operator ☎ **03**
Telekom directory enquires in English ☎ **11837** (toll call)
Telegate directory enquiries (in German, but cheaper) ☎ **11833**
Country codes:
Australia **00 61**
Canada **00 1**
Ireland **00 353**
New Zealand **00 64**
UK **00 44**
USA **00 1**

Bicycle rickshaw in the city.

Time Difference

Munich is on Central European Standard Time, one hour ahead of GMT in winter and two hours ahead in summer. It is generally six hours ahead of New York and nine hours ahead of San Francisco.

Tipping

Token tips for doormen, chambermaids, cabbies, etc. are expected. In restaurants, although service charges are included in the bill, around 10 per cent tip is usual, unless the service has been miserable.

Tourist Information Offices

Munich's tourist office has its headquarters at Sendlingerstr. 1 ☎ 233 03 00. There are also offices in the main rail station, Bahnhofplatz 2 ☎ 23 33 02 57, and on Marienplatz in the Neues Rathaus (New Town Hall), ☎ 23 33 02 72/3.

For information concerning travel in Upper Bavaria (skiing, Ludwig's castles), get in touch with the **Tourismusverband München-Oberbayern e.V.**, Bodenseestr. 113, D-81243 München ☎ 829 21 80.

The German National Tourist Offices abroad can also provide information:

Australia Lufthansa House, 12th Floor, 143 Macquarie Street, Sydney 2000, ☎ (0123) 673 890

Canada 175 Bloor Street East, North Tower, 6th Floor, Suite 604, Toronto, Ontario M4W 3R8, ☎ (416) 968 1570

UK 65 Curzon Street, London W1Y 8NE, ☎ (020) 7495 0081

USA Chanin Building, 52nd Floor, 122 East 42nd Street, New York, NY 10168-0072, ☎ (212) 661 7200

11766 Wiltshire Boulevard, Suite 750, Los Angeles CA 90025, ☎ (310) 575 1979

Tours

The Munich Tourist Office offers, or can organise, tours of any length and on any theme. There are standard tours offered by travel companies such as **Panorama Tours** (☎ 54 90 75 70), which take visitors round the major sights in a large air-conditioned touring coach, walk them through the Old Town or the Alte Pinakothek, show them Munich at night, and so on. The **Stattreisen e.V.** (☎ 54 40 42 30) emphasises certain themes on its tours, which are usually conducted especially for children, with travel on the trams (see also **Bicycles**).

One very special way of touring Munich is by **rickshaw**. Sometimes the drivers wait at Marienplatz wearing their sharp yellow shirts, otherwise you can call **Rikscha Mobil** ☎ **129 48 08** or **(0171) 287 30 32** (mobile).

Trade Fairs

Trade fairs are held at the International Congress Centre Munich (ICM) located to the east of the city where Riem airport used to be. The organising body is **Messe München GmbH, ☎ 94 92 30 23**. The Chamber of Industry and Commerce can also supply information, ☎ **51 160**.

Transport

The **Münchner Verkehrs- und Tarifverbund (MVV)** operates the city's buses, trams, underground trains (U-Bahn) and city trains (S-Bahn). The extensive system as a whole is very well organised. The network operates until 1am, but special bus lines run until around 4am to make sure the night owls can get home safely. Maps of the train system are available at MVV outlets at U-Bahn and S-Bahn stations. Fares are calculated according to the **zone** you are travelling in. There are four zones in all, but the first one already goes slightly beyond the city limits. For example, if travelling on a *Streifenkarte* (multiple-trip ticket) with 10 strips (DM 15), you have to cancel two strips per zone. From Marienplatz to the airport you would cross four zones, hence you would have to cancel eight strips. For short trips (maximum two U-Bahn or S-Bahn stations or four bus/tram stations), you only need to punch one strip, but you can only travel for one

Triple tram.

hour. You should cancel your ticket by inserting your *Streifenkarte* into one of the low blue boxes near the escalators that go down to the track.

The MVV offers day cards, but better still for visitors is the popular **Welcome Card**, which not only allows for unrestricted travel within the first zone until 6am the next morning, but also gives you discounts on bicycle hire at Radius Touristik, on entrance fees to many museums, to the IMAX cinema, the Zoo, and so on. The Welcome Card also comes in three-day versions and in three-day partner versions for up to five people, two of whom may be older than 18 years of age, for DM 42. The Welcome Card is available from the Munich Tourist Office, and wherever the München Welcome Card sticker is exhibited.

Children under 6 travel free, and from 6-14 years of age they can use special children's tickets. The U21 tariff is for 15-20 year olds, who buy the adult strip for DM 15 but only cancel one strip per zone.

Bicycles can be taken on the S-Bahn and U-Bahn either for the same price as the person or with a day ticket for bicycles. Bicycles are not allowed on the trains during rush hour (Monday to Friday 6am-9am and 4pm-6pm).

Taxis: Taxis either drive around town, or wait at hotels, the rail station or at officially designated stands. As long as the light is on, they will stop (assuming the driver is not on his or her way to pick up a fare). Calling ☎ 216 10 or 194 10 will generally summon a taxi to your doorstep within ten minutes. You can also order taxis for the next morning or for later on the same day/evening. Drivers will extend their service to sight-seeing, long-distance drives, transportation of goods, and the cab company can even organise limousines, minibuses and piloting. A drive out to the airport from the main train station can cost up to DM 90.

TV and Radio

For English-language broadcasts you must either rely on various satellite channels, such as CNN, or twiddle the dials on your radio. In the evenings, the BBC can sometimes be caught at 648 AM (evenings), otherwise try SW at 6195 or 9410. Voice of America has a strong signal at 1197 AM.

INDEX